MW01171337

By Our Testimony & The Blood Of The Lamb

True Stories of God's Warriors

By Richard L. McBain
Contributing Authors
Douglas Raine
Gary Vanover

Printed in the United States of America
Triune Group Publishing
Copyright © June 6, 2022
All Rights Reserved

ISBN 9798835225095

Richard L. McBain

Our Testimony & The Blood Of The Lamb

Contents

Prologue

Belief in God's existence through faith and commitment to His Word is what causes men and women to step out in obedience and unabashedly share the Gospel. Everyone who calls themselves Christian has an obligation to spread the Word in a way that each personality can express it. Some are shy and find it hard to evangelize, and that's okay. Personal "Witness" is a form of evangelizing whereby one shows what they believe by a Christian example of living. Others are outgoing and find it much easier to speak out about their faith in Jesus the Christ.

The true stories in this book are actual testimonies in narrative form that show us all of some real warriors for Christ. Many have a direct calling to go and take the Word of God to those who have never heard, and in doing so put themselves in dangerous situations. Others talk to friends and neighbors in telling them what God has done for them in their lives. Some do charitable work for the under privileged, while others give to support ministries who are out doing what they can't. All of these are forms of evangelism.

Our Testimony & The Blood Of The Lamb

The Bible in Revelation 12:11 says that we overcome "By the Blood of the Lamb and the Word of our testimony." Some people have told me that they really don't have a testimony, to which I reply, "So you've never done anything for the Lord in your life?" When they answer, "Yes I have," I say. "Well that's your testimony!"

Great or modest, each of us has a testimony that begins with how, when, and where we got saved. From there we can add any Godly supernatural happening in our lives or just what we have done for the Lord. Maybe it's participating or even teaching a Bible Study in church or at home, or even being a prayer warrior who prays for the needs of others.

Once saved we all have the "Blood of the Lamb", so now we add whatever out testimony is to that, and we become overcomers. I hope you enjoy the stories given, and that they will encourage you to step out when and where you are able.

Richard L. McBain

Section One
Testimonies of Douglas Raine
A Director of Full Gospel Business Men's Fellowship International / America

Mission Trip To Cuba
November 18 - November 24, 1996

Our Plan was to go to Pinar Del Rio, Cuba, but God's Plan was for us to go to Havana, Cuba. We were given the day, time, and strategy to go to the University of Havana. Many months of preparation for this trip originated in prayer and continued for the entire trip. We would like to personally thank those prayer warriors at the First Baptist Church, Commerce, Texas for their dedication in lifting us to the Lord.

Three people would be representing our church in Cuba; Dr. Bobby Tollinson, Dr. John Moss and Douglas Raine. We were to meet up with Dr. Ralph Bethea in Nassau on November 19, 1996. Dr. John received his passport just hours before our departure, and his wife Betty was gracious enough to drive us to the Waco Airport. We were ready and excited to see what Jesus was going to do.

We met Dr. Ralph Bethea in Nassau and our entry into Cuba was just in sight. We were able to tell others about Jesus on the flight into Cuba. Upon arrival into the Havana Airport we held our breath as we were trying to get by Customs. We had two boxes filled with religious literature - 1 box containing 800 gospels of St. John and 1,500 tracks in the other box. Other boxes contained medical supplies, and toiletry items. Two of the immigration inspectors sought permission from a supervisor to allow the literature in. Once through Customs we were able to make contact with a few born again Cuban believers.

We waited two hours for a government approved taxi to go to our destination, and we were soon to learn the laws of the land. Little did we know we were not supposed to speak to Cubans, have Cubans act as interpreters that were unauthorized to do so, and definitely not stay with Cubans. The government is strict and wants all foreigners to stay in government hotels; ride government approved vehicles, and maintains a respectable distance from the Cuban people.

The four of us stayed with the Garcia family in a small concrete home surrounded by fruit trees and they all had the love of God in their hearts. Three generations of families lived in this dwelling; the grandparents, the parents, and two children. However, the one child was a young adult whose formal name was Jose Garcia which was nicknamed Ouche, who acted as our friend and interpreter. Ouche was an air traffic controller.

As we arrived there were three other missionaries; Pat Still, Jay Franks, and Dennis Garrett who were all from the Nashville, Tennessee area. They were there one week prior to our coming and had many stories to share of Cubans coming to Christ. They were primarily working through the mission churches which were based from a mother church, being along established Methodist church.

The three from Nashville were extremely excited as they shared what Jesus was doing in the lives of the Cuban people. This is a country where God is not allowed and freedom of worship must be done under cover. The mission church pastor that they followed was Ivan Suarez who was on fire for the Lord. Our initial thoughts were to continue the work of these three and then journey to Pinar Del

Rio which is about a two and a half hour drive southwest of Havana.

The following day we met with the church leaders and found out that they had been watched very closely and had received a letter from the government that they would be closing down mission churches. They were afraid for us to get involved with evangelizing the Cuban people for fear of losing their church. Christianity in Cuba is being won an inch at a time.

There are many informers in the nation of Cuba and the Cubans are always looking over their shoulder. We learned that they could be severely persecuted for following Jesus Christ, because Cuba is an atheistic nation. The Cubans can lose their job, home, be imprisoned, and lose their food allotment. The government rules by fear.

After leaving the local hotels, we decided to go to the Marina and witness. Dr. Ralph Bethea and I took translator Miguel Rio to the West Sea Wall and Dr. Bobby Tollinson and Dr. John Moss went with Marlene to the East Sea Wall. There were scattered police around the area and Ralph and I began to witness to the people. One was a bus driver with a companion who was waiting on passengers to look over the Marina. They listened to what we had to say but were constantly looking over their shoulder in fear of being spotted.

The passengers were beginning to board and the two men excused themselves and left. Both were computer specialists at the harbor and one knew a little about the Bible. Ralph and I went to the next group on the Sea Wall. After over an hour of discussion and witnessing the gentlemen who could speak partial English accepted Jesus Christ and the other asked permission to be allowed to read the gospel of St. John before he asked Jesus Christ into his life. Miguel our translator was very enthusiastic as we witnessed. However, Marlene was afraid to translate for Bobby and John and thus had to abandon their evangelistic outreach.

We decided to see a little bit of the city and journeyed out to see old Havana. The police were very active and stopped our driver Abner. The initial fine set at $65, but with continued discussion Abner was able to reduce the fine to ten pesos which amounts to about fifty cents. God's sovereign protection was with us. Abner is a medical student and is in his last year of medical school along with Miguel Rio. Once the two graduate from medical school in July they will make $20 per month. Both Abner and Miguel were always on the lookout for police and informers. We went back to the Garcia's to plan for the next day.

Thursday morning we all piled into Rene's 1958 gray Chevy Impala and were off to University of Havana. The plan was for Rene to drop us out near the university and pick us up at five o'clock. We were equipped with about 800 gospels of St. John and around 1,200 to 1,400 tracts. We split up in pairs as we went to the university so as to not attract attention to ourselves. That was almost impossible since I am about a foot taller than most of the Cubans and neither Ralph nor I were able to speak any Spanish.

As we tried to enter the University from the south side we were blocked by soldiers and not permitted in. Thus we began to walk around the campus and prayed for God to bind Satan, the powers and principalities of darkness, and prayed for the blood of Jesus Christ to be over the University. We asked that Jesus show us the way in and there it was, a stairway leading into the University from the east side of the campus. We climbed a flight of steps and entered into a courtyard and found ourselves right by campus security.

Ralph went out to scout the campus and to devise a plan of action. Upon his return he said that he had never seen security there such as this. Soldiers with AK47s were positioned every thirty feet a across the campus. Our plan was to hand out all the information in ten minutes and run. This sounded like a good idea, however it would be impossible to hand out over 2,000 books and tracts in that allotted time.

Ralph looked at me and said, "Maybe we're not prayed up enough." As we began to go up into the campus John was to go with Ralph and Bobby and myself were to cover the East, North and West sides of the campus. This was the first time in my Christian life, I felt fear, but the Holy Spirit brought scripture to comfort me in Acts Chapter 4, and the verse which I heard audibly gave me courage. The Holy Spirit said, "It is better to obey God than man.," and my legs that had been frozen began to move quickly. God's timing was perfect, but we would have preferred it not be so intense.

The University was lined with Mercedes carrying various country flags in the front. Educators from all around the Caribbean, Central and South America, and educators as far away as Holland and Israel were attending a conference. Leaders of other nations, taxi drivers, and students all received the gospel. The four of us were carrying back packs which were loaded with tracts and the Gospel of John. Our pockets were jammed full as we moved about campus.

I found myself in the center of the campus in a Greek revival structure. I was in the center of the educator's conference and found myself about to be put under arrest. I was surrounded by security and could feel the gun barrels pressed against my body. They were yelling at me in Spanish, but I couldn't understand one thing that they were saying perhaps ignorance is blessed. One short lady who approached me was the Conference Leader who spoke English. She said, "Are you on holiday?" Immediately I knew what to say, "Yes, I am on holiday." I was asked to leave and the security stepped back. Once out of sight, I continued to handout tracts and the Gospel of John in Spanish.

That night I asked the Lord why I wasn't taken to jail. The Holy Spirit replied, "My work was not done." I began to cry in bed as I realized that God made my escape possible because I had only handed out half of my witnessing tools at that point. I thanked God for allowing me to serve Him.

The people were very respectful and all thanked me for the gifts. One young man looked up at me with tears of joy and said, "I am a Christian and God Bless you." A young coed grabbed my hand with smiles of delight for she had read the tract and became a believer. She wanted tracts to pass out her friends. I could feel the spirit of God moving, and I could see how God could use ordinary men to do extraordinary things. Two young ladies came running to me and had prayed to receive Jesus Christ.

We distributed all our literature and could see the students, faculty and others intently reading the message of our Lord and Savior. John, Bobby and I gathered at the pre-assigned rendezvous location and shared our experiences as to what Jesus was doing. We continued to wait for Ralph to return.

Around 12:30pm, we saw Jose and his mother coming onto the campus to get me. They had our airline tickets. God led them directly to us.

Upon my return with new airline tickets in hand, I told Bobby and John that they could go to lunch while I waited for Ralph to return. As I waited at the foot of the steps a young working lady approached me by the name of Gamile. She was an attractive young lady with coal black hair, brown eyes wearing shorts and a low cut tight fitting top. She stood about chest level and was trying to proposition me, but my intent was to tell her about Jesus.

After about ten minutes of standing and getting nowhere, we sat down on the steps and I tried to tell her about Jesus using sign language. All I could think of is that I wished that I had retained at least one Spanish tract so that I could share it with her. With exasperation, I looked up and Bobby and John were standing there. Bobby sat down next to her, opened up a tract and led her through scripture and a sinner's prayer.

That afternoon Gamile's name was written in the Lamb's Book of Life. We told her who to contact at the nearest Baptist church so that she could be discipled, then she went up the road. Five to ten minutes later she returned with her boyfriend. We went through the tract again, and they looked at me and smiled. They wanted to know what we had written, and how they might be discipled in Jesus Christ.

We grabbed a young Cuban who could speak some English to interpreted for us. I wanted them to look in the phone book and they walked away. We learned later that Cuba had not had a telephone directory since 1959. Some of the people had phones and we prayed that they would find the church. What a beautiful thing Jesus can do in one's life.

We circled the block and went back to the steps leading into the University from the North side. John, a retired college professor, was too tired to go on. At the foot of the steps people began to come up to us as we shared the gospel. Two young boys who were nine and ten years old could read and understand the tract. Trying to communicate with them proved to be fruitless and they spoke no English and we spoke no Spanish. Then some Cubans which could speak some English appeared and we began to share Christ with them.

Right before our departure from the campus an Israelite from Tel Aviv said that he wanted to visit with me earlier, but was rushed for time. He saw me handing out tracts. The Israelite's name was Arturo Lopez Levy. He indicated that his tribe was priests. We began to discuss the Old Testament proclaiming the God of Abraham, Isaac, and Jacob. We discussed the prophets, Moses, Samuel, David, and Isaiah. He had to rush to class, as he was already fifteen minutes late. As he departed, he said that he would love to continue the discussion and gave me his phone number. He indicated that there are two Jewish Universities in the United States; one in New York and the other in Cincinnati, Ohio. He hoped to get on staff in Cincinnati.

The next day we visited the University of Havana, and the military wasn't present. We counted three hundred to four hundred students that claimed to receive Jesus Christ.

As our time drew near, we journeyed back to the rendezvous site only to find out that Ralph wasn't there. It was a half hour to forty minute drive back to the Garcia's by car. We met John Hamilton, a missionary from Tulsa, who joined us at the Garcia House. We prayed for Ralph's safety, and at 6:30 pm we received a phone call from Ralph. Miguel Rio was going to pick him up, and we could hardly wait to hear Ralph's story.

Ralph arrived just in time for dinner. We hugged him and were overjoyed to see him. We sat down to eat dinner and listen to his story. Ralph was also handing out tracts on the southwest side of the campus when a group of students surrounded him and inquired about Jesus Christ.

Any type of gathering draws the police and Ralph found himself under arrest. He tried to communicate with the police, but to no avail. They were about confiscate his tracts that he had placed on a railing intending to use them as evidence, but he slowly moved away from the tracts and the police moved with him. Out of the corner of his eye, Ralph could see the students take the entire stack of tracts and distribute them among themselves. The police looked over for their evidence, but it was gone.

Ralph was off under escort to the police station to

undergo interrogation. Many of the detectives tried to accuse Ralph of selling literature on campus and holding money back from the government. He was able to convince them that no money changed hands, and he was ushered into the assistant police commissioner's office. Once again Ralph went through interrogation, but this time with a different result. The commissioner asked Ralph, "Why is an educated man like you doing this?" Ralph stated that it was out of his love for the Cuban people that he wanted to share the love of Jesus Christ with them.

Carlos Tones, the assistant commissioner invited Ralph to go to his house. Along the way the commissioner discussed his daughter's condition with Ralph. As they arrived at the commissioner's house, Juanita, the commissioner's wife, greeted Ralph with much enthusiasm and said that she had been praying for him to come to their house. They went into Suzanna's room, the daughter of the assistant commissioner, and found her to be doubled up lying in bed with severe stomach pains. She had been in this condition for two months and was only able to take nourishment through a straw.

Ralph prayed over her and when finished, Juanita,

Carlos, and Ralph went into the dining room to eat. While eating fried bananas, Suzanna walked into the room with tears flowing down her cheeks and walking over to the table and she sat down to eat. This was the first time she had been out of bed for two months. Juanita began to cry and Carlos was also bleary eyed. They had seen the power of God touch and heal their daughter.

Shortly thereafter Ralph led Suzanna and Juanita to Jesus Christ. Carlos too wanted to accept Jesus, but said that he had done too many bad things to have Jesus in his life. He said, "I kill Christians." Carlos told Ralph that he was extremely grateful for the act of mercy His God had for his daughter. Carlos made a promise to help us. When you break our laws, I will protect you.

As we looked back over the chain of events, Jesus Christ orchestrated our entire activity from the beginning to the end. We all sat down and cried. We experienced the power of God that day.

We gathered together with the Garcia family and the rest of our newly found Cuban friends. It was a time of joy. Jose showed me a sheet which was dated in 1990 which were coupons for clothes. He asked if I would like to have a coupon to get some clothes from Cuba. It was a big joke; there were no clothing stores to redeem the coupons. They would wash and mend the few clothes that they had. The only clothes that they received were those coming in from America by organizations who were trying to help the Cuban people.

I will remember this trip for the rest of my life and look forward to the time I can return to Cuba and share the gospel of Jesus Christ with a people that have no hope, no dreams and no future. The Garcia's gave us their rooms, their beds, their food and extended the greatest hospitality we could ever expect. Our meals consisted of rice, chicken, beans, and lots of fresh fruit and juice.

On our last night they killed a lamb which was truly a big sacrifice for them. We paid the Garcia's ten dollars a night for the room and ten dollars for meals. The entire three generations of the Garcia family stayed in a bedroom and slept on the floor. I asked Jose if the money helped and he said, "It was incredible." It made all the difference in the world. They work for nothing and have almost nothing to live on. The house that we stayed in was quite comfortable; however, they had many obstacles to overcome as the house desperately needed repair.

The dining room had many little ants which nested in the outlet receptacle, and a three inch lizard poked his head out the other outlet. It was quite entertaining to see everything moving about and being extremely busy. The bathroom area was self-contained with polished granite that was pilfered from one of the hotels. The shower system had only cold water, however an electrical heating device was placed in the head of the shower unit warming the water so that it was quite comfortable.

The power coming into the entire house registered at about 106 volts. Laundry was done with a washboard and clothes were ironed with a vintage iron. Even when they used equipment which was fifty years behind us, they were still neat and clean. The rooftop of the house was brick tile and was slightly sloped. Cisterns were over each bathroom and were filled sometime during the day by a government pumping system. Up on the roof was a vineyard while the main trunk system rose at least twenty feet in the air before being trained to the trellis canopy. The grapes were quite easy to pick, but were poor quality.

Jose's grandfather maintained an orange orchard of about 2,400 trees. This allowed for fresh fruit and the growing season appeared to be year round. At the back of the house was a large lime tree with about a half-acre of banana trees and mango trees. Underneath the fruit trees were chickens, a goat and a lamb. Behind the house was a large field in which two workers with an ox plowed the ground to plant tomatoes. The goat was used daily for milk and fresh milk was provided each morning, and it was easy to be spoiled as each morning and each evening we dined on fresh fruit.

Jose's Uncle was Castro's private pilot and flew the Cuban president to the Vatican in Rome to visit with the Pope. While Castro was busy visiting with the Pope and showing that he was interested in opening Cuba to religious activities, it was quite the opposite on the home front. As I mentioned earlier Castro's government was busy closing down mission churches and trying to stop any growth of Christianity.

The Cubans do not use toilet tissue. They use they hand and a little pitcher of water to clean themselves. The porch furniture was made of iron which was forged in the form of rocking chairs and regular straight back chairs. They were extremely comfortable and during the evening the family would visit on the porch using the cool breeze coming off the Caribbean to cool them. It was fun to watch frogs walk across the top bar of the fence and listen to the evening sounds.

It was hard to believe that just one block away were row houses side by side with no front or back lots and a very modest porch which almost came out to the street. Those which stayed at home would spend most of the day out on the porch watching the people go by. The Cubans were in much better .shape than we were because they either walked or rode a bike everywhere they went. It was common place to see girls out hitch hiking for rides. Miguel said that it was perfectly safe for girls to hitch hike
in Cuba.

Ralph Bethea on a trip that he made almost a year ago asked one of the government officials as to what was the single greatest thing that the communist government brought to the Cuban people. After a moment of thinking, he replied, "It has made eleven million thieves." The people exist on the black market. What you have today someone else might have tomorrow.

One of the ladies that we met had fallen through a corrugated asbestos roof over a car port. She broke her arm, skinned herself quite severely and hurt her hip and heel. We anointed here with oil and prayed over her. She thanked us for praying. In discussion with Miguel, the hospital was handicapped by lack of literature, lack of scalpels and suturing equipment, lack of beds and mattress covers, and no operational sterilization equipment. Miguel indicated that the conditions in the hospital were anything but desirable, but they would always do their best to try and help the people. The government supplies free medical service to the people.

Five years later we learned that our initial seeding of the gospel at the University, created 1435 underground churches. PTL

A CALLING BY THE HOLY SPIRIT TO NICARAGUA FULFILLED IN 1999

While walking through the Oklahoma City airport

in 1992, a man walked up to me and said that I would be going to Nicaragua to minister. My initial thoughts were that Nicaragua was in civil war and that would be the last place I would want to go.

As the years passed, the Holy Spirit began to put a love in my heart for the Nicaraguan people and a desire to go there. There was a prophecy given over Nicaragua which stated: "There are yet four months and then came the harvest. Behold I say to you lift up your eyes and look on to the fields that they are white for harvest." Thus the timing of God would be in the months of April and May in 1999, in which people would come unto Him.

The scripture showed me as to what God would be doing. In Joel, Chapter 2, versus 27 through 29, states: "Thus you will know that I am in the midst of Nicaragua and that I am The Lord Your God, and there will be no other, and my people will never be put to shame. And it will come about after this that I will pour out My Spirit on all mankind, and your sons and daughters will prophesy. Your old men will dream dreams, your young men will see visions, and even on the male and female servants I will pour out My Spirit in those days."

The vision given to the Full Gospel Business Men Fellowship International was a God-like vision that was to take a nation for Jesus. Plans were being made to be a part of this movement of GOD and I flew to Nicaragua on May 3, 1999.

Of course the enemy knew what was coming and the week before my arrival, the airport was closed due to rioting. The government increased gasoline taxes which resulted in a major bus and taxi strike. The strikers were enraged, demonstrated violence and crippled the area. They would tear up the roads, burn tires in the middle of the roads, etc. Thus people could not get to school, go to work unless they walked, road a bike, a horse or drove a car.

There was great anger expressed by the strikers. We recognized this as an attack from the enemy and began to pray. As we did the strongholds were coming down. We arrived in Managua, the capital city of Nicaragua, on the evening of May 3, 1999. Nationals picked us up to go to a dinner. The dinner was on the other side of town, and of course none of the Nationals that were driving me spoke English. Once there, they assigned me a gentleman by the name Marvin Castillo, a National who said that he was giving a week to God.

Marvin was experiencing tremendous leg pains which also was a reason why he was not working. As we prayed for Marvin, God healed his leg. I also had an opportunity that evening to lead his wife to JESUS. And as the week progressed, I was able to lead his brothers, his mother, and his entire family to Jesus. Many that evening came forward for prayer for family problems and the Spirit of God was ministering to all.

This war-torn country was in the midst of recovering from the horrors of war. Homes would have surrounding walls towering fifteen-feet tall with barbed wire on the top. It was amazing that as each individual gazed upon the walls, we all received the same picture from God seeing that the enemy strongholds would come crashing down.

This story itself unfolds from the Book of Joshua. This is the time after the Nation of Israel had spent forty years wandering in the wilderness, and was prepared and ready to go into the promised land.

God told the leaders of the Nation of Israel that the city of Jericho was theirs. Even though the walls were tall and thick, they had God's promise of victory.

At God's command the men of Israel marched for six days around the city of Jericho once. On the seventh day they marched around the city seven times, and on the seventh circling the priests were to blow seven ram horn trumpets with a long blast, and the men of the Nation of Israel were to make a great shout. Supernaturally the walls came down and they entered the city and declared victory.

Satan and his demons had held captive the country of Nicaragua. We knew that our struggle was not against flesh and blood, "but against the rulers, against the powers, against the world forces of this darkness, and against the spiritual forces of wickedness in the heavenly places." We would put on the full Armor of God and bind these foul spirits of darkness, rendering them helpless because God had promised victory.

Fire Teams of ministering servants were set up to go throughout the land. Our first mission effort was in an inner-city school called, " Villa Flor," of around three hundred students. Fire Teams went into each classroom to share Testimony and declare the Gospel. I could sense hindering spirits of learning in the classroom, and we were able to bind and take authority over the suppressive forces and allow the Spirit of God to touch everyone.

Every student and teacher received Jesus that morning as their personal Lord and Savior. We instructed the teachers to pray over the chairs of each student prior to the start of class. Students would come up to me and through translation state that they felt dumb and could not learn. God is the source of wisdom and knowledge, and we prayed over the students to receive this power. I believe in my heart that the students that came for prayer, and were once rejected and criticized will be the leaders of tomorrow.

From there we moved to the Intercontinental Hotel in which I had an opportunity to minister and evangelize to tourists, businessmen, a sports hero by the name of Dennis Martinez, and to the Vice President of the Country, Enrique Bolanos, and all were receptive to Jesus. In the Intercontinental Hotel lobby I was also able to visit with a Roberto Calderon, a man who learned English because he was a drug trader. It was only one month before our arrival, that while on the beach under the influence of drugs and alcohol, he heard the Gospel of Jesus Christ.

His life was changed and he had not indulged since meeting Jesus. I asked Roberto (who was translating for Richard Chittrarr, the President of the Full Gospel Fellowship International) if he had received the Baptism of the Holy Spirit. He said that he had not and I prayed for him and he received. He was so excited that God could use such a sinner as he in His Army. Our ministry continued on into the evening!

On Wednesday we would be leaving the city of Managua and traveling to a village called Nandaine, which was located 65 kilometers southeast of Managua. The man heading the teams for the area was Carlos Canales, a former officer in the military. My translator Marvin, was born here in Nandaine. He said that he could sense and see a change in the people.

We were taken from house to house to pray for the sick and to evangelize to the businessmen in the marketplace.

One of the homes we went to was the Alvarez home. There were three generations living under the roof. There was a lot of concern over the granddaughter, Juniet Maria Alvarez Talavera, a dear sweet little girl who was losing her eyesight. The family showed me a paper from the doctors explaining the eye disease and that there was nothing they could do. We were asked for permission to pray and we could feel the presence of God.

I removed her coke-bottle thick glasses after we prayed, and I handed her a Bible and asked her to read. She read continuously an entire page and did not miss a word. God had sovereignly healed her. It was exciting to see what Jesus was doing as we continued from house to house praying for people.

While crossing through the market square, I was attacked by a man who desperately needed money for alcohol and drugs as he was going through withdrawal pains. One of the Salvadorians came to my rescue and he said to the man that we will give you money if you pray with us. He was lead in the sinner's prayer and a change came over the man's life. Only God can reach people like that!

Next we went to the public school where the
Youth Group made a dynamic drama presentation
of the Gospel, shared testimonies, and offered the
Plan Of Salvation. About eight hundred students
came forward to receive Jesus Christ as their
personal Lord and Savior, and all of the teachers
came forward as well. At first I was praying with
one at a time and quickly being encircled we were
praying with four, five and six people at a time.

The teachers also needed Jesus and received Him.
It was tremendous to see what God was doing. A
lot of ministry continued to take place and
continued up into the early morning hours. While
ministering that evening, there was a young man
whose last name was Rocka, who had been blind
in his left eye since birth, and his mother, Rosarco,
had Lupus. As I began to pray over him, the Holy
Spirit knocked him down and his head and face
were spastically shaking.

I felt in my spirit that that was the healing power
of God. I personally did not find out if God had
healed this young man because I was surrounded
by the people who needed desperately to have
prayer for them. At the end of the day we saw at
least a thousand people come to Jesus Christ in

Our Testimony & The Blood Of The Lamb

Nandaine, Nicaragua.

Thursday continued ministry and ended with a town dinner in Nandaine. Testimonies were given and ministries performed. God was answering prayers and performing many signs and wonders, and many also received the Baptism of the Holy Spirit.

Our journey home was not without incident. We were stopped by Sandinistas in the mountain area and were lined up against the cars. I thought at first that they were going to shoot us. The Brotherhood bowed their heads and prayed, and the Glory of the Lord fell on the soldiers, and they all received Jesus.

Friday new doors opened as we were back in Managua. Marvin, my translator had to work that day and I teamed up with two Salvadorians, one Guatemalan and one Nicaraguan. I was fortunate to have John Cgilrekk of Guatemala) and Jaime (of Salvador), who were fluent in English. Our first stop was a police academy on the west side of the city. We met with a prisoner who was on his knees praying. He was a member of the Fellowship, but had overdrawn his account and was thrown in jail.

This man was able to join us as we witnessed through our testimonies to the police. Everyone in the academy received Jesus. After that they asked who would disciple them and we pointed to the prisoner and said that he will disciple you. From there we journeyed to a military post only to find out that we could not get in. We then lead the sentries and guards to Jesus which enabled us to set foot on the post.

It was amazing to see how we received favor and the eagerness of all to received Jesus. It was now time for lunch and a time to relax. After lunch we began to meander through the city and ended up at a radio station, 580. Over the next two hours it was incredible as to what began to happen. They sat me down and shoved a mike in my face. I was able to share prophecy and the love of God.

Jaime Sol tapped me on the shoulder outside the radio station and said the Lord has just revealed something to me." As Jaime looked at the couple and said, "You have 9 children from 9 different women and the woman you are living with is not your wife. And little girl you have a spirit of unforgiveness." Then Jaime said, "Okay Douglas you can take over." Both were crying and repentant and prayed to receive Jesus. The daughter who was about 12 years old had a deformed leg. I laid hands on her and immediately her leg was healed.

During our time on the radio people were beginning to line up outside of the station for prayer. It was amazing, and I found it amusing as I looked through the window of the broadcast room into the public area in which I watched one of the ladies continue to push the big hand of the clock backwards so as to enable us time to present the message.

The entire staff at the radio station received Jesus Christ as their personal Lord and Savior. We then began to pray for the people coming to the station. The first one was a man with prostate cancer, the second was a young girl of eleven years old who had an extremely sweet spirit. She had one crooked undeveloped leg and was continually in pain. Her leg was beginning to be healed and straightened.

Five years later I returned to Nicaragua and asked about the couple. He was the biggest drug dealer in Nicaragua and Costa Rico and now he owned the

largest rehab centers in both countries and had
morning Bible studies in each center. The man had
joined the Fellowship and went from chapter to
chapter to tell his story.

One of the men, who was a Director in El Salvador
for the Fellowship, received a discernment of
spirits -- lust, unforgiveness, etc. This girl's father
had nine children by nine different women and this
needed to be dealt with. As we began to pray, both
father and daughter were completely broken in
spirit and were able to forgive one another. This
was truly a touching moment.

Our time was up as we now had to go to the east
side of Managua to go to one of the government
agencies which dealt with animal and aquatic
human resources and environmental issues. A man
and his wife shared their testimonies with the
group. A salvation call was made after the
testimonies and all received Jesus. This was
exciting because they wanted to start a Chapter of
the Fellowship right there in that very area where
they received Jesus.

We regrouped and traveled to the other side of
town where we met to share what God was doing.

Members of the Fellowship from other Central, Latin American countries, the U.S., and South America shared some incredible stories as to what God was doing, and ministry continued afterwards.

Saturday, we ministered in a large marketplace, not like our supermarkets, but many shops selling paper goods and other items. This area was jam packed with shoppers. More ministries took place until the time that we were to meet at the coliseum. A lot of prayer went up on behalf of the Nicaraguan people for the touch of God to be upon all.

One girl who I had prayed for to receive her hearing, was cornered on the front steps entering into the coliseum. She was prayed for by a lady of the Fellowship and anointed with oil and received her hearing. Even with one hearing aid one ear was completely gone. However, the healing power of the Lord Jesus Christ opened her ears so that she might be able to hear, and we all rejoiced.

Many were coming to Christ and being healed and prophesized over before coming into the coliseum. It was very difficult to keep track as to what God was doing because miracles and salvations were occurring every minute. In our brief week's activities of evangelism, there were more than ninety-seven thousand (97,000) recorded salvations. Ninety-seven (97) eye healings were recorded.

Thank God for the many, many new found friends in Nicaragua and other countries. This truly is a picture of the Body of Christ. Working in unity and with one spirit, we made a difference!

In 1997, our Full Gospel Businessmen's Team Ministered in Budapest, Hungry

We passed out fliers with stories of healings by Jesus and the apostles. There were two men who were Hare Krishna followers that became Christians. The only thing that they knew was that which was printed on the flier. They came across a beggar at the train station, and they read from the flier and repeated the words said by Peter and John. They fastened their eyes on the beggar and said, "Silver and gold have I none; but such as I have, give I thee: In the name of Jesus Christ of Nazareth rise up and walk. They took him by the right hand, and lifted him up: and immediately his feet and ankle bones received strength. They were on each side of the beggar walking slowly, then faster, into a slow run, and praising God.

The news media (local newspapers, radio and television) covered the story. The man (beggar) was telling everyone to come to the park and meet the men that knew Jesus. Revival was breaking out at the park as the citizens of Budapest came to see the man that was healed. Many were praying to receive Jesus as Savior and Lord, and many were filled with the Holy Spirit as evidenced by speaking in tongues. The joy of the Lord was everywhere.

I met these two men again at another outreach in Budapest in 2004. They were wearing suits, had hair, and were proclaiming the Gospel. People were receiving Jesus and the Baptism of the Holy Spirit. Our team traveled with these men all over Hungary meeting with businessmen, community leaders, and gatherings of Gympie's. Many areas didn't have churches, but these men had setup Full Gospel Chapters and were mentoring men in the faith. A few of these areas had over one hundred thousand people with no churches. Molnar Miklos was then the Full Gospel President of Hungary

MINISTRY IN UKRAINE
May 9, 1999

Ukraine President opened up the doors to the country, Kiev - Bible distribution, with an attitude similar to what NYC had done in a different Crusade: Many Christians traveled to see us, and one who I led to Jesus Christ in August 20,1999 thanked me for leading him to faith in Jesus. Two teams would be in the Battle room every morning.

May 10

In the City of Cherkassy there was the Christian Mayor over a city that had a sweet spirit. There were thirty decisions for Jesus in the Cancer Hospital; people who had no hope. Ninety percent accepted Jesus, and we prayed for the sick. They asked the question of, "Why would a God of love let us suffer." There was a man who was a Muslim, who was too sick to read. He accepted Jesus, and many non-believers would stop us and come to Jesus. We prayed over a lady and she rose up praying in tongues giving all the glory to God. We believe she was healed.

The city was very receptive to the gospel. Thousands turned out for the crusade, and we worked in the crowd and bonded with the people.

We were sad to leave when it was over. A colonel in the Army, who was in charge of a prison, set up a chapel in the center of the prison. We witnessed to him two years earlier and he prayed to receive Christ. The government removed him as warden. I asked him why was he here, and he said I am now the Chaplain over five prisons. Hundreds of teenage boys received Jesus, and there were many reports of miracles. I received a plaque because of my Christian witness. Never have I felt the compassion of the Holy Spirit so strong in the Ukraine as in Cherkassy.

May 11

Driepropetroski was a city where only Russian was spoken, and only recently were visitors allowed because they made bombs there. This city had a demonic stronghold of control and fear. Only one of five of our translators for our team were Christian. We visited an orphanage which had only two to three year old babies. All were dressed alike and well behaved. They loved to hold your finger or to be picked up.

May 12 & 13

We went to Sevastopol which was a Russian naval base. We distributed Bibles and witnessed in a market there. The year before we only had Ukrainian bibles and the people would not take them, however many came to Jesus. This city had been rebuilt after WWII. We witnessed and prayed over a blind man who had seventy-two operations and never saw his son and he was confused about the truth. He thought Jehovah Witnesses, Mormons, and Islam all worship one God. We told him that Jesus is the one and only true God, and he said he never felt such love.

Later that evening this man was sitting on the curb and someone was reading the Bible to him. Street kids and people of all ages were drawn to us. Many (about 50) prayed with me to receive Jesus, and in turn would return a gift. (Lenin pin and other pins,. a lighter given to me by a young girl.) They were excited to receive Jesus Christ.

Yalta - Marcus Hester preached at a Baptist church and was stopped by Misha, who was responsible for one hundred plus churches in Ukraine. His reason was that the translation being given was not correct. We continued to minister and distributed Russian Bibles in the town and park. Many of the people spoke English, and there was great excitement about Jesus. Many pictures were taken with new believers. We fortunately had no run in with Mafia as opposed to our trip in August 1999.

MS vendor received Jesus, and a lady who wanted a one dollar received my lunch and the bread of life. As I went back to the bus for more literature and Bibles, a lady ran out to greet me. We prayed over two young (18) deaf men, and the Spirit of God came over the one who initially rejected me. When Jesus came into their lives they were changed. **Odessa** had been ruled by Germany then Russia. Lenin killed 41 million Ukrainians to bring them into submission, and thirty percent were Jewish.

A Ukrainian Gideon leader took us to an Asylum on the south side of town with very few people. Marcia prayed hymns on the flute, and only about sixty came to Jesus, of which thirty were youth playing basketball nearby.

In 1998 the mayor of Odessa would not let the people off Riverboat II until the President said to the mayor "let the Americans do anything that they want to do; they are here to help our people." Oxanna, a high school English major was serving as an interpreter. Her mother was a teacher, and had not been paid since February, and her father was a merchant marine. I met her father, a 2nd Engineer on the flight from Frankfurt to Kiev. It was her father who I had placed a track in his pocket before he went to jail in August '99. This beautiful young lady would be going to the University to learn English and business.

At the train station our Indianapolis team distributed sixty Bibles in less than one hour. One young man, a Russian Orthodox missionary that I met on the street, translated and helped me minister to the people. His question to me was, "Why were the Baptists persecuting the Orthodox?" The only answer I gave was that we were there to exalt and proclaim Jesus.

Prayer opened Odessa. We went back to the boat to get more Bibles and to witness on the street where many more came to Jesus. The Crusade that we had that evening was rewarding. A Jewish believer brought a friend who accepted Yeshua as his savior and was born again. LaVerne walked up and I said this is my wife and she received a big hug. When it was over we were Sad to leave.

Kherson was a city that six teams evangelized, while two teams went north to Nikolayev, a city which was off limits to visitors until 8/21/91 when there was independence. This city built nuclear submarines and was still well guarded. We went to a nursing home there having about three hundred residents. After witnessing most hands went up to receive Jesus, and many lined up for prayer who had headaches. One lady from Poland had been uprooted and transplanted there. She could not speak Russian or Ukrainian, and had a spirit of torment, and we prayed for her peace.

When we went to the City Market, and many came to Jesus. We distributed fifty Bibles and thirty prayed to receive Jesus. Women wanted Voice Magazine, a publication of the Fellowship for their husbands, and one came back with her husband. Many men had become alcoholics and were bitter over work because many times they would not get paid giving them no hope! Some wanted to know if Jesus could deliver them. One man would get mad and walk off, then would come back to hear more about Jesus and the truth. We ran out of Bibles and tracks and continued to lead people to Jesus.

We went back to a Baptist church where we left our team leader, Marcus Hester to preach. The Holy Spirit moved over the people, and many got healed and the Assistant Pastor received the Baptism of the Holy Spirit.

At our Crusade in Kherson, we worked the crowd and many were coming to Jesus. Electricity was in the air, and I bonded with two men in the crowd; Nickoli and Sasha. Jesus was the bond, and again it was sad to leave.

Zshapparozoha's city market was a place we went to witness, and we had about forty decisions for Jesus there in one hour. My wife LaVerne found me by following a trail of excited new believers. Mac Brunson, Pastor of FBC Dallas came to get me as two young men had just prayed to receive Jesus. One vendor got so excited that she kept giving me sunflower seeds. Randy reported that one lady gave him her shoes in appreciation. As one would come to Jesus they would act as a recruiter, and bring their friends and family. The local pastors were greatly encouraged. The Plant in Zshapparozoha, is in an industrial city with heavy pollution. Over five thousand there received Jesus, and even our crew in the Riverboat got saved.

Orphanage MS - Bunny Martin, a YoYo Champion, gave a message of rules and punishment. Nickoli Senior and Sacha a 4th grader helped Marcus who gave a chair illustration and faith in a wheel barrel, which was a tremendous evangelism principle. The Government had let the church operate the orphanage who taught that they must trust in Jesus. They were poor and had nothing. Afterward we went back to boat.

Kremanchuk

We waited on the south side of the bridge for three and one half hours, and we began to pray for the bridge to open and it did. Our team was bused to an orphanage (only 22 kids) which was surrounded by apartments. I stayed by the bus to witness to the community. Forty-three came to Jesus and our group distributed five thousand bibles in one hour. That evening many came to Jesus, and we ran out of bibles. Question: How do you handle different denominations? Answer: Love them. We are Christians first. Question: How do you treat cults, such as Jehovah Witnesses, etc. Answer: Treat them with love and lead them to Jesus.

Kannya

Our translator, Shevchenka came from Cherkassy. The town honored the great poet Taras Scevchenka, and was a clean affluent city. The Indianapolis team went to an orphanage of four hundred kids, and all wanted a personal relationship with Jesus. The children were well behaved, and seven hundred Bibles were distributed with ministry. We finished for the day in Kannya the heavens opened up and the rain fell.

Kiev

The next morning we went back in Kiev. We ministered to vendors and handed out one hundred and fifty children's tracks. We then flew to Frankfurt, Germany and took the train to downtown Frankfurt. At our second stop thousands of happy football fans crowded on the train. We needed Bibles and tracks, and no one spoke German. Robert Steel wanted to preach, and LaVerne wanted to give them a Bible. Western Europe needs Jesus Christ, and we unfortunately realized that there were many Satan followers in Frankfurt.

Summary:110,000 bibles distributed; 13,000 recorded decisions for Jesus. 85,000 tracts, and numerous new friendships. Sad to leave new friends.

Closing:
America can listen to the gospel every day; whereas the Ukrainians have had eighty years of communism, and a nation without God. They are eager to hear the gospel.

Amos 8:11- Behold, days are coming," declares the Lord God when I will send a famine on the land, not a famine for bread or a thirst for water. But rather for hearing the words of the Lord.

Is. 42:20 You have seen many things, but you do not observe them, your ears are open, but none hears.

MAY 18, 1980 - Mount Saint Helen exploded with a great force straight up into the atmosphere and sound waves went out in intervals. This explosion could be heard for a distance of 600 miles and rocks and debris were found 200 miles away. However, the people around the mountain heard nothing. Scientist called this the dead zone. We are a nation living in the dead zone. We can go to church and not hear the good news of Jesus Christ. My prayer is that American's desire the Lord with the same enthusiasm as our Ukrainian brothers and sisters. Has God brought a famine to America?

El Salvador- October 23-26, 2000 Full Gospel Business Men's Marketplace Outreach
Initial Obstacles (Reported by Melanie Meza)

One week before the outreach was scheduled we hardly had any meetings setup, and we seemed to have no support. Nobody seemed interested, and the Lord reminded us about the moment when Demos came to him asking if he should go on with FGBMFI. The Lord asked him, "Will you ever doubt My power?" The Lord then gave us a word in Proverbs 21:31, "The horse is made ready for the day of battle, but victory rests with the Lord."

We declared ourselves incapable of doing anything but pray. Luis and Melanie de Meza drove through the city of San Salvador and asked the Lord to take control, and they rested and waited upon Him. The next week we had more than a hundred people coming from Nicaragua, more than one thousand meetings setup, and about forty-eight thousand people were reached with the Gospel. Isn't the Lord amazing? Will you ever doubt His Power? The Lord has showed us a way to approach businessmen; it is by His power that those people were reached. May your eyes be open and may you clearly listen to His voice, and may your heart be open and humble for Him to show you a new way of reaching souls.

Welcome to El Salvador

The Lord is pouring out His Holy Spirit on El Salvador. Upon our arrival in El Salvador; we were met by Jaime, a friend that I worked with in Nicaragua. Our team from the USA compromised of John Schmook from Arkansas, Tommy, Jim, Lloyd from Oklahoma and George Duggan from Charleston, SC. Eric joined us the following day from Tacoma, Washington, and Grace Smith joined us Thursday evening from San Antonio.

Wednesday afternoon we traveled up the side of a volcano to Jaime's grandmother's house which overlooked San Salvador. The gardens were beautiful, but our purpose was to pray over the city and ask God to turn the indifference of the people's heart back to Him. Everything begins with prayer.

The Holy Spirit was setting up meetings all over the country while we were praying. In fact, the City of San Miguel had eighty meetings planned during that time. That evening I went to a meeting at the Radisson and three businessmen received Jesus, and we then had ministry.

Thursday morning we had a breakfast meeting at the Maya Country Club. I shared my testimony and handled the ministry. I had a vision while praying for a pastor in that I saw a building going up, and I didn't have a clue what it was about. Later Thursday the team travelled to San Insulatan after our breakfast. The team split with the Americans going to a school, and I went with the Salvadorans to a military base.

First the officers and NCO's listened to testimonies from Col. Armando Anaya of the Fellowship. The thing that impressed me was the faith of the base commander in Jesus Christ. His name was Colonel Herbert Ouijas. Two of us shared with about 300 to 400 troops. After my testimony, I led the ministry and we all prayed the sinner's prayer, with many that came forward for individual prayer.

The Holy Spirit was strong as I prayed for some soldiers to have courage and to fear not, and they were then slain in the spirit. As I looked over at the Commander, he was praising God for touching his troops.

We then went to city hall where the Mayor had gathered the staff and we shared testimony with about two hundred. After my testimony, I handled the ministry, and almost everyone prayed to receive Jesus, and I called for the people to come up to receive their miracle. The line was long, and after two hours the Americans showed up to help me with ministry as it was getting dark. God is good!

On Friday we travelled to Ahuachapán (October 20). We went to a textile factory, and they would bring forty women in at a time to hear testimony. Our team, Jaime, Eric, Grace and I rotated as other groups were scheduled one right behind the other. About three hundred prayed the sinners prayer and while one group was listening to testimony, ministry was going on outside. Many were afraid of losing their job as the company had shut down the thread line.

God was changing and affecting lives. We drove up into the mountains to have lunch. In the afternoon we had a meeting with the Health Ministry in Ahuachapán. Twenty-three prayed the sinner's prayer and some came forward for special prayer needs.

On Saturday we had a morning meeting at JAQUELINE CAROL, a manufacture of hand and face cream. Melanie de Meza scheduled this meeting. About forty people, ten men and thirty women were in attendance. All prayed and twenty-five came forward for individual prayer. Grace and I shared testimony. We prayed for solutions to family problems and health.

At noon we were at a computer shop where Eric shared his testimony and I handled the ministry. Eight prayed to receive Jesus, and three needed special prayer, including the owner who had Lupus. The owners previously worked for Texas Instruments (TI), but when the executives of TI were being kidnapped, they closed the plant. We had ministry in two shopping malls and prayed the blood of Christ over two businesses selling Halloween costumes.

Later in the afternoon we went to a pawn shop where I was the only American. We shared testimony with fifty men and one woman. The lady was the General Manager (GM) and a strong Christian. Garcia opened with testimony and I closed with testimony and ministry. Many were in sin and were looking for the easy way out. One man received prayer for his hearing and the GM asked for prayer for her children.

That evening we went to a concert at a soccer stadium to hear Marcus Witt. The message was for Latin's to take the gospel to the entire world. The music was great. In the morning we went to church and the priest taught on missions. It was the same theme as last night- Salvadorans need to take the gospel to the entire world. We met up with the rest of the Americans at a country coffee plantation for lunch and fellowship. We were very busy the rest of the week.

Monday October 23, 2000
We went to a school in a poverty area. Peter, a young Salvadorian shared his testimony to 40-45 students in grades 7-11, and I did the ministry while Hector Mayorga translated. In the afternoon we travelled to the town of Opico, where we were

to meet with the police department, but the meeting was never established. The chief of police was out investigating a complaint in the marketplace, and the second in command would not make a decision, and asked us to wait.

Waiting is not one of my spiritual gifts, and so Grace Smith and I went to the marketplace to pass out tracts and share the gospel. The people were receptive to answering our questionnaire. Grace could speak Spanish so we worked as a team and when we were down to our last two tracts, we gave them to a police woman and street vendor. I asked for three minutes of their time, and l asked them if they were going to heaven when they die. The officer was very attentive and prayed to receive Jesus. Grace did a great job as the Holy Spirit revealed Jesus.

As I looked up our evangelism team was gone, so we went to the police station and right behind us was Inspector Sofia Gonzales, the chief of police;. It was Sofia who just received Jesus. The police were not interested in us speaking with them, but they had a change of heart when the chief gathered her staff to listen to our testimonies. Jaime, our leader said that the officers were making wise cracks as they filed into the room. l shared, and then Eric and I closed. As the Holy Spirit revealed Jesus, all twenty-three officers prayed to receive Christ; God is good.

Monday evening we had a meeting at the Holiday Inn. Eduardo Quinonez who owned a shoe business, was the Chapter President. Doctors, businessmen from El Salvador, Nicaragua, Costa Rico, Panama and America were present, plus the country's Prime Minister and other dignitaries. It was a meeting of who's/who. Raine and Bolivar Gomez of Panama shared testimony and I did the ministry. One doctor had a spirit of pride. He was a plastic surgeon who lived in El Salvador and Paris, France.

Another surgeon came forward and wanted the emptiness in his life filled. While his wife in the next room was listening to Grace Smith's testimony, she accepted Jesus. A police inspector who was also a police academy instructor received a blessing. I prayed for the Prime Minister to receive wisdom and favor with the courts.
On Tuesday, October 24, we went to a bilingual school, Colegio Euroamericano. Both Grace and I shared testimonies and I closed. Abraham of the

FGBMFI was there to help. Seventy students plus ten teachers prayed to receive Jesus. The principal, an ex-priest, gave us full reign. No one came forward for ministry, but the head master said that the students wanted to speak to us at break time.

We ministered to five groups who came with their peers from the same grades 7, 8, 9,10 and 11th (seniors). One group were committed Christians who were seeking wisdom on how to serve God and how to witness to their friends. They did not have anyone to disciple them.

We drove to Santa Ana to drop off a suitcase for Grace. Her son-in-law who was running an Assembly of God Seminary in Guatemala was sending someone to fetch it. We passed out eighty Bibles and one-hundred-fifty tracts in a nearby mall. A policeman stopped me and said that we could not distribute anything. I told him that I could not speak Spanish, and he let me go. What was interesting was that we had handed out everything just before he said that I couldn't do that.

Our next stop was a shirt factory, American Park in Teca. It was almost dark when they were having a shift change. There was a wave of people coming through the gate as we distributed 300-400 tracts. Later that evening we did deliverance on Abraham.

On Wednesday October 25, Hector Mayorga and myself went to a school named Instituto Cultural Oxford. Roberto Alvarado owned the school and welcomed us. There were sixty-three students plus teachers and staff. They were attentive during my testimony and invitation.

The school is in a poverty area and many of the students had low self- esteem, anger, gender problems, single parent families, masturbation problems, etc. We prayed with Roberto for a break through. The school has to follow many of the same standards as the USA; such as, teaching evolution and not creation. Discipline and short attention spans created learning problems.

Mid-morning we went to a children's hospital that they called The Hilton. About twenty people on two teams of ten ministered to doctors, nurses, staff, patients, relatives of patients and all received Jesus. As we prayed for the sick, the Lord was performing miracles by removing fevers and lung problems. Doctors would stop what they were doing and receive Jesus. There were twenty-two floors in the hospital. Next we went to an annex building about two blocks away and did deliverance ministry.

We had lunch at Wendy's and upon leaving; Melanie asked the manager if we could share our testimonies with the employees. We were the only ones there and I called the workers together and asked them if they were going to heaven when they died? I led them in the plan of salvation and they prayed to receive Jesus. Immediately after they prayed, people started coming into Wendy's. It was a divine appointment.

That afternoon we went to a soap factory, and many received Jesus Christ. There were religious spirits in and around the place, and a person entered the meeting with a demonic spirit. I asked who this person was, and Melanie said he was a witch doctor. The spirit of witchcraft was bound and we were able to continue with the meeting. Upper management was not there. Melanie and I were disappointed because the owner was her father and brother.

We anointed their desks, chairs, and lockers with

oil and prayed. Melanie's step mother had a hindering spirit and a negative influence on her father towards God.

On the Campus Universidad Tecuologica de El Salvador had nine thousand students and the faculty prayed to receive Jesus. The owner of the school was a FGBMI Member.

Thursday morning Luis, Lazarus and two other Nicaraguans shared testimonies at an export company with thirty employees. The owner's husband had been shot and killed and she was a strong believer. The employees prayed to receive Jesus. During our ministry time the Lord was directing us in what to pray as we prayed for the needs of the people.

Lazarus asked me what our chapter was doing to reach the lost. I said we have been working with the Dallas chapters and had seen about 1900 come to Jesus. I said it with a spirit of pride. Then I asked Lazarus, a former communist colonel in Nicaragua, what his chapter was doing for Jesus. The answer that came from his mouth humbled me and I felt ashamed as he said 16,000 had prayed to receive Jesus. It was only a month ago that I led many of his neighbors and relatives to Jesus. God is sovereign.

On the plane ride home, two passengers on my left prayed to receive Jesus. The one closest to me said that he felt good and was going to call his wife in El Salvador when he got to San Francisco with the good news that he was Born-Again.

CHINA - MISSION OUTREACH BEJING, CHINA
January 15-22, 2002

Our objective was to Prayer walk, encourage believers, build relationships, and witness. We had to appear as tourists, and began our Prayer-Walking by praying on site with insight with Steve Hawthorne and Graham Kendrick.

Our Team 17 had Christians from many denominations that came under attack from the enemy. The people had dental pain and problems, headaches, eye problems, and stomach disorders. Their prayers removed infirmities and health was restored, as the Team performed in one accord.

The history of Beijing, China, the Capitol of China, had a population of twelve million people, and was originally founded in 1200 AD. Beijing had three recognized Christian churches; two Protestant and one Catholic. It began with the Shun Dynasty 2230 BC -246BC, where they worshipped one God , The God Of Heaven (Discovery of Genesis by CH Kang & Nelson)

The Chen Dynasty 246BC burned ancient classics and records, and over the next 49 years introduced other gods and redefined religious vocabulary, becoming more mythical. Buddhism was introduced in 67BC, but with caution. China has become a Communist country where it was against the law to openly evangelize, but if we were asked what we were doing we could share Jesus.

We worked with a underground church, and left them praise music, a guitar, and Bibles. Next we prayed while walking at Tiananmen Square. Then on Monday we prayer-walked in the Silk Market and other Markets in the area where merchants were all business and very aggressive.

On Tuesday Marty and I prayer walked in a park near the Hotel-Ding Guang New World Hotel. I distributed my testimony, listened to men's folk singers, listened and participated with choir, and witnessed. Government officials came to observe what we were doing. Handing someone a tract could land us in jail.

We prayer walked on the wall and on the wall was a spiritual wall, not made with stone and mortar, but the sins of a nation layered on each other reaching toward the sky, and the blood of the innocent was crying out. The more I prayed for China, the more I felt an urgency to pray for America. I prayed for God's forgiveness starting with me. The indifference of America toward sin will surely bring judgment on us, so we must repent.

JORDAN/IRAQ TRIP NOVEMBER 2003

Twenty-four people from nine different states traveled on this exciting ministry journey to Jordan and Iraq. The ministry was divided between working with the churches in Baghdad and ministering to Iraqi refugees in Jordan. The team raised funds to give away 11,000 New Testament Bibles to the Iraqi people: 8,000 for Baghdad and 3,000 for the refugees. Later part of the New Testaments were traded for complete and children's Bibles upon the request from the leaders of the Iraqi congregations.

Ministry in Bagdad

The teams visited 5 different churches of various denominations. Among them were Assembly of God, Presbyterian, Christian and Missionary Alliance, Church of England, and a Catholic Church. Many new churches were started in Baghdad. One of them led by pastor Gassan Thomas was only three months old and ran three hundred people in attendance.

The team also visited an orphanage run by Catholic Nuns. The children at the orphanage had lost their parents in wars, Saddam's prisons, and other calamities. The nuns said that they could stay at the orphanage as long as they wanted to. Along with the Bibles the team provided a month's worth of groceries for the orphans.

One of the girls, Mina, had an especially touching story. A Muslim family who immigrated to Germany adopted her. The family tried to convert Mina, a Christian, to Islam. Unable to cope with the pressure she escaped, miraculously found her way back to Baghdad and came back to the orphanage. One of the team members, a retired preacher from Illinois, was so touched by Mina's story he vowed to adopt her.

Not knowing whether they would have contact with the US Military, many of the team members had one thousand letters of support for the American soldiers. The team was able to meet and have breakfast with the Army Chaplain, Colonel Wismer, at the former Saddam Hussein's palace.

The Colonel took the team on the tour of the palace, and according to the Iraqi people, Saddam Hussein had exclusively Christians as his palace staff. He trusted Christians and tried to win their sympathy by sending flowers and greeting cards to Christian churches on Christmas and Easter. However, if a Christian attempted to evangelize they were thrown in jail.

The Pastor of the Assembly of God Church in Baghdad spent three months in a 2m X2m cell with no windows, sharing it with six other people for telling someone about Jesus. Our interpreter in Jordan, Iraqi refugee Yad, was tortured in Saddam's prison for giving someone a Bible.

The team members were approached by many

Iraqis telling them that the people of Iraq are very thankful to President Bush for freeing them from Saddam's regime. They said that they are praying for the American soldiers daily.

Winning the Muslim people to the Lord is a task that will take patience and perseverance. Showing them "Christian love in action" by tending to their physical needs along with the spiritual ones is the most effective way to minister to them.

FGBMI made a commitment of ongoing involvement in the ministry to the Iraqi people by giving them the Word of God, and simultaneously providing their physical needs of food, medicine and medical treatment.

Ministry to the Iraqi Refugees

At that time there are 400,000 refugees from Iraq living in Jordan. They escaped the wars and the brutalities of Saddam Hussein's regime, yet they found themselves stuck in Jordan, unable to work, provide for their families and often unable to move to another country. They don't receive any financial support from the Jordanian Government. The Jordanian Alliance church reached out to the refugees by hosting a dinner, where as many as three hundred of them showed up.

During the service prior to the meal Pastor Yusef Hashweh gave an invitation to receive Jesus Christ. All the Iraqis stood up to pray the prayer. This is how the first refugee church started. Today there are a number of them spread across Amman, Jordan. Many Muslims come to these churches because through their food distribution program and free medical clinic they can receive free groceries and medical treatment. This has proven to be a great evangelistic tool; "Love in action".

Every two months the Alliance church gives away two hundred $30 coupons to the refugee families to buy rice and other basics. Every Monday the free clinic treats several hundred patients. Our team was able to pray for the patients as they waited for their turn. Many of them were Muslims, yet they gladly agreed to be prayed for.

In Jordan the team had given away three hundred fifty New Testament's, three hundred fifty full Bibles, and three hundred fifty Children's Bibles. We also provided over 500 meals along with the Bibles. The President of the Jordanian Bible Society, Jamal Hashweh, has expressed gratitude to the team for coming to encourage the Jordanian Christians. He shared how tough it is to live a life as a Christian in a predominantly Muslim country. He also shared about the lively Bible distribution that is done by the Bible society throughout the Countries of the Middle East; Morocco, Saudi Arabia, Tunisia, Syria and Sudan.

MINISTRY IN MANAGUA 2004
October 19 - Tuesday-Arrival at 6 pm
Our Hosts were Roger and Luisa Gonzalez, and we stayed at the Hotel Casa Blanca. Our USA Team Members were Edgar Gonzalez, Maria Williams, David Smith, Alan and John Schmook, Milie, David Boyce, and Douglas Raine.

Oct.20- Wednesday- Meeting with National FGBMFI Leaders at FINEC office in Managua. Reunion with old friends, Marvin Castillo, Lazarus, Eddie, Alberto, Humberto and about thirty new friends were made. Team assignments were posted at the FGBMFI Headquarters location by type of business and name, contact, etc. Upon return we listed how many we saw and how many prayed the sinners prayer of acceptance. In our **Outreach Primary School DRR Testimony**, fifty students gave a testimony in each classroom.

Vo-Tech-Testimony had two classes with forty students; three individuals on campus made decisions.

Luncheon: Holiday Inn- thirty prayed to receive Jesus and two prayed to receive the Baptism of Holy Spirit. We later had a meeting with chapter leaders.

Oct.21- Thursday- Seminar AM; Chapter Breakfast at Princess Hotel. I led a candidate for Mayor, Nidro Marenco of Managua, to Jesus in the entrance to the Princes Hotel.

Jail in market–We gave our testimony to thirty-three prisoners and twelve guards. Several guards had AK-47s on the outside of the fence.

Seminar in afternoon
We had a Chapter dinner at Nagarote with testimonies and fifteen decisions for Christ were made. We then had other meetings at Café Jordan, Plancha(youth), Jinotepe, Dirioma, Masaya.

Oct.22-Friday- Fire Teams worked at Chinandega, Leon, Esteli, Masaya. Friday Evening we gave testimonies at Cornerstone English School to two hundred fifty students, then had dinner at Chinese-WOK Chapter Meeting where seventy-five attended and fifteen decisions were made.

Oct.23-Saturday- We had a Chapter meeting at Crown Plaza DRR and David Boyce gave his testimony. There were salvations and ministry. We then setup a meeting with some military, which was adjacent to hotel. Next we went to the Radio Station and gave testimonies over the air. This was at the same station we were at in May 1999. We then had lunch at the Tennis Club.

Oct.24-Sunday- At breakfast Lazarus gave his testimony, and there were fifteen decisions for Jesus. We then went sightseeing at a lagoon in L.de Managua, and we received a gift. Next we went to Granada where we took a boat ride on Lake Nicaragua. Later we went to the Fellowship Dinner at Hotel La Ceiba in Los Isletos.

Oct.25-Monday Lunch in the market(68 acres) at Restaurant Quque Landia; three were saved. We distributed one hundred twenty-five tracts in the market, and people would even run after me to get a tract.

Oct.26-Tuesday- Long Outreach Program from 4am to 1am in Matagalpa with fifty-two meetings producing five thousand two hundred decisions for Jesus. Among them were:

1. At a coffee exporter's company, Commodity Group Inc. Carlos Javier Mejia was the President and the interpreter was Jorge Salgado. There were thirty-three saved.

2. At a Grade School testimony was given, and class salvations were over one thousand.

3. At Lunch at the Coffee Plantation-Selva Negra-DRR gave testimony to farm workers, and thirty-seven prayed.

4. At a College Miguel Larreynaga gave testimony with the School-Interpreter, Jorge Salgado and thirteen teachers prayed.

5. University Del North –DRR testimony to 52 people with fourteen decisions.

6. Candidate for Mayor of Matagalpa, Horacio Brenes gave his testimony, and forty prayed.

7. One Hundred fifty tracts were handed out on the street.

8. Chapter Dinner with David Smith giving his testimony, and fifteen decisions for Jesus were made.

9. We also had a large healing and deliverance ministry.

Oct.27-Wednesday- We visited a village near the San Juan River close to San Juan del Norte. Warren one of our interpreters (lived in Bluefield's) To get to the village it was four hours by car, then four hours by horse and then two hours on foot (near Costa Rica). FGBMFI Chapter uses testimonies from the radio station that we broadcasted from. A Witchdoctor attended the meeting, renounced witchcraft, burned all his demonic books, received Jesus and the Holy Spirit. I prayed for this Chapter President in San Marcus. The people have to rely on God because they have nothing. They see and experience God's miracles.

Nueva Guinea
We did Street ministry during the open time, and distributed one hundred fifty tracts, and ten prayed to receive Jesus. Dr .Rodriquez and I traded shirts. We returned home on October 28, 2004.

TRAVELING PROTECTION 2005
In February 2005 I was traveling west on Highway 239 between Goliad and Kennedy, Texas. There was an 18 wheeler in my lane, and I started to pray in tongues. Just before impact the driver swerved to miss me, hit the grass on the other side of the road and darted back behind my van. The truck

and trailer rolled 6 times before coming to rest near a utility pole on its side. I turned my van around to go help and continued to pray in tongues.

The driver was dangling from his seat belt, and I couldn't get to him. There was a four inch tear in the roof so I put four fingers of my left hand through a tear and ripped the roof off. I entered the truck cab and could not feel a pulse or respiration. I carried him to safety and when I laid him on the ground God raised him from the dead. I said to the driver, "God must really love you." Then I heard God say, "Tell them about Me."

A crowd began to gather and were screaming, "The truck is going to blow." I calmly re-entered the truck through the roof and turned off the ignition. I returned back to the man who was standing and talking to the crowd. I was shaking and amazed how God protected me, gave me wisdom and strength to do the super natural, and gave the truck driver new life. I had a captive audience to tell about God's love. I continued my journey as my adrenalin began to return to normal, and I felt pain in my hand. It was lacerated, and I thought about how my Jesus suffered for me.

MEDAN INDONESIA, SEPTEMBER 2005

The "Fire Team Outreach" in Medan, Indonesia was very successful. Our brothers in FGBMFI at Medan were helpful, organized and operated with a sweet spirit. The Lord had given us a vision for Medan, Indonesia - John 4: 35 and Joshua 6. On Sunday September 11 we saw the ones dressed in white. They were Muslims sitting around the Mosque in white robes next to the mall where we were going to eat after church. Jesus would be drawing them to Him.

The story of Jericho was seen in the spiritual. The walls around the city and through the city were high and prayer would (spiritual warfare) bring down the walls. The Lord prepared the way to penetrate and take the city and He would receive the glory.

The churches and FGBMFI work very well together in Medan. All of the Pastors wanted to hear about the vision and we received to bring the message to the flock. The events surrounding our visit were changing the lives of the people. The morning of September 9, a Mandala Airlines Indonesia flight from Medan to Jakarta crashed on

79

takeoff. We arrived at Medan on Malaysia Airlines that afternoon. One hundred seventeen people were killed on the plane and thirty-two more on the ground.

Medan is 60% Muslim and the Governor, Tengku Rizal Nurdin, and two members of Parliament were killed in the crash while going to visit President Susilo. The regional government was represented by three Muslims and one Christian. After the crash Dr. Rudolf Pardede, a strong Christian, became Governor and two Christian representatives were added to the Parliament changing the representation in Parliament to three Christians and one Muslim for North Sumatera.

On Saturday September 17 , John Schmook, myself, Paulus Rianta, Richard Saragih, and Paul Wakkary met with the Governor and his wife for three hours. We received favor, prayed and listened to the Governor's plans looking toward "The Great Commission."

The region to the west, ACEH, had been at war with the Indonesia government for three decades. A cease fire and peace agreement was signed in Finland while we were in flight to Indonesia. The

peace monitors from many countries were given
training and assignments at our hotel,
just before the Asian-African Convention in
Bandung. Radical Muslim groups, Islamic
Defender Fronts, and the Anti-Apostasy
Movement Alliance were responsible for
blockading and closing forty Christian churches in
Jakarta and Bandung.

A 1969 ruling stated that churches had to obtain a
permit from the local authorities and permission to
build from local residents. The Jakarta Post
reported that churches applied for permits, but
were rejected by Muslim officials. Christian
lawyers were going to appeal this law to the
highest court in the nation. This was the catalyst
required to stir God's people.

An FGBMFI Fire Team Training Seminar was
given to the Directors, Field Representatives,
Chapter Presidents and members Monday evening
September 12. The Indonesians met for prayer
after the seminar and received the vision from the
Holy Spirit. Meetings were scheduled at
businesses, universities, and for University
Christian Leaders (Campus Crusade), a college,
hospital, drug rehab center, churches, hotels,

prison, restaurants, FGBMFI meetings for all the churches, FGBMFI Banquet Rally, etc.

Many received salvation, the Baptism of the Holy Spirit, teaching of God's Word, healing and deliverance. God touched thousands of people, and I will tell of one of the healings that took place at Methodist Hospital.

A male patient had surgery to remove cancer of the throat. His voice box was open to receive air. When I asked if we could pray for him he had great fear in his eyes and facial expression, but consented to receive prayer. As we finished praying he stopped breathing and within seconds the cancer and infection shot out of his voice box. It came out with such force that it startled me and the smell of the disease and infection was strong and pungent. The fear left this man and a great peace came over him as he prayed to receive Jesus.

Gideon Esurua joined us for two days. He greatly added to the ministry of the "Fire Teams." Voice magazines were enclosed in Sunday's addition of the Jakarta Post and sent to the nation. The paper also devoted a full page to Perubahan Masa

Depan's testimony. Our brothers in FGBMFI continued the work in the city of Medan with four million people, and spread the "Fire" to the nation. Jesus has opened the door to claim and take the city for Him. We were blessed to be a part of this outreach.

OUTREACH TO MEXICALI, MEXICO, AND CALEXICO, CALIFORNIA, APRIL 2006

Forty-one businessmen from Texas, California, Arkansas, Honduras and Mexico met in Mexicali, Mexico to introduce the city to a Man that changes lives. We took this message to businesses, hospitals, ranches, schools, and two chambers of commerce, restaurants, parks, government agencies and officials, politicians, hotels, and people on the street.

Television station 66 and local news media covered the events. Over four thousand people heard the message of hope and responded. Additional activities of the week included a dinner which introduced church leaders of all Christian denominations to FINHEC, and a barbecue lunch was provided for city leaders and businessmen.

We had a ground breaking ceremonies and a dedication for "The Campus of Hope;" and concluded with a celebration in the park. Thousands of needy people gathered in the park to receive food, the message of hope, the Gospel of John, miracles, and great entertainment. When Richard Shakarian asked the people if they needed a miracle, every hand went up and the FGBMFI team prayed for every person.

FGBMFI partnered with TRIUNFO for this special celebration in the park. The needy people enjoyed the music, clowns, puppets, and dancers, which contained the message of hope. Free haircuts, manicures, medical and dental exams, medicine, eye glasses and love were given to the people.

Family members would ask team members to come and pray for loved ones that were unable to come to us. One little five year old girl by the name of Vanessa had broken her foot and her mother asked for prayer. She was so shy that she buried her head in her lap as we prayed for her. We never saw her face until her mother whispered, "look at the clowns" and she lifted her head and smiled with great joy. Everyone was ministered too and smiled and were very thankful.

Lives were changed and people were delivered and filled with the Holy Spirit. A visit to the local detention center proved to be fruitful. Prisoners were released from their cells except for one inmate that didn't want to hear the life changing testimonies in the courtyard. The response was incredible. The man in the cell also heard the testimonies. Just moments before he was vocal and was swinging around in the cell like a little monkey, but as we were leaving he too wanted to receive this Man. He went from being demon possessed to freedom in Christ.

The powerful testimonies at the barbecue drew many successful businessmen to the Savior. Obstacles of getting the food and Gospels of John across the border proved to be challenging, but character building. But after a week of trials and much prayer the food arrived the night before the distribution. The physical and spiritual needs of the people were met. Praise God!

ARMENIA AIRLIFT 2006

The preparation for this Airlift was a lot of Prayer, Partnerships with Missionary Adventures International and local Armenian Churches, fund raisers, Marketplace Teams (Fire Teams) and Full Gospel Business Men's Fellowship in America. Our theme was from Demos Shakarian's Gospel Tent Crusade.

We gave a slide show, one being of Noah's Ark from Genesis 5:29-9:29 and resting on Mount Ararat. Another slide was about the Nations surrounding Armenia. Then a presentation of Market Place Ministry, Airlifts, and Fire Teams given by Douglas Raine, John Schmook, Edgar Gonzalez, Jesse Cradduck, Nils Petersen, and Brad Stine.

Next was a slide of Khor-Virap Monastery, and Gregory the Illuminator, which has been shared in Demos Shakarian's book, "The Happiest People on Earth." As the presentation went on we talked about business people who have a vision for Armenia, and are bringing it to pass through fresh ideas and commitment.

The whole purpose of this was about assembling an Airlift Team for Armenia. We needed to develop relationships with business and Church Leaders, and establish FGBMFI Chapters in Armenia. We also needed to conduct Business

Seminars, Assist CAI with Evening Tent Crusades, and target Businesses, Government Agencies, Universities and Training Institutions, Hospitals, Prisons, Police Authorities, Military Bases, Community Organizations, and Embassies.

The Airlifts objective was to evangelize the people, educate the leadership, and establish Chapters. The Fire Teams involved with the Airlift needed to provide visitation, vision, and invitation. We also needed to train Chapter Leadership in procedures and building membership.

The Gospel Teams were led by Christian Adventures Joint Venture Ministers in tent evangelism. The Team was made up of Dr. Kevin and Leslie McNulty, Armen and Melania Gasparyan, Akop (Jacob) Mkrtumyan, Kirill and Olga Kozorez, Yauheni Hurynovich, and Gala Lefshyna.

Next the "Demos Shakarian Gospel Tent" program, in cooperation with Christian Adventures International's 2006 Gospel Tent Crusade, put the "Shakarian Gospel Tent" into permanent service for the nation of Armenia with an Armenian evangelist, and dedicated to the founder of the

FGBMFI, all in conjunction with the Airlift. New converts were given the opportunity to join a local church and become a member of a local Chapter of the FGBMFI.

Demos Shakarian Tent Crusade - Yerevan, Armenia 2006

We (Full Gospel Business Men's Fellowship) were invited to partner with Drs. Kevin and Leslie McNulty of Christian Adventures International for a tent crusade in Yerevan, Armenia. There was tremendous support from the evangelical churches and pastors. Our Fellowship Founder, Demos Shakarian, was well known and respected by the citizens of Armenia.

During the day we would conduct business seminars in the tent, and the evening we would host the crusade. The Holy Spirit surrounded the event as five thousand people attended the event the first night. Armenian choirs opened with worship, and I was invited to speak before our keynote speaker Dr. Leslie McNulty who delivered the message in Russian. At the end of the message, an invitation was given to those who were healed of deafness to come forward and testify. Thirty people came forward. A man was healed who had no ear drums. Many came forward for prayer. The crowds grew over the next two nights. One family came from Iran to receive a touch from God. The government authorities shut down our crusades on Wednesday.

We were sending teams to minister on a local television stations and evening dinner meetings. Pastor Arthur Simonian sponsored a dinner meeting of fifty-two business leaders. After the meeting, I stepped outside to thank God for all the healings. I heard the Holy Spirit say, "Armenia will be a light unto the Middle East. " As I looked up, I could see a glow over Mount Ararat, and then He said, "Make disciples." I countered with, "I will only be here a few more days." And He put on my mind the Internet. I said, "You will need to teach me." Thus Full Gospel Businessmen's Training LLC. was birthed.

We have developed a great relationship with the Armenian Church and business leadership over the last thirteen years. One of the large churches I ministered in, I asked, "How many people have read "The Happiest People On Earth?" About eighty-five percent of the audience raised their hand.

Other parts of the Armenian Airlift presentation were regarding the need for Business Visitation, and Good Samaritan Meat Production. Business Acceleration Seminars by Yerevan, and at Emanuel Church for four Days conducted by Yerevan, then the Gospel Tent for three Days. The need to visit Universities and schools was part of The Center for Leadership Development Mission Statement: To equip and develop a new generation of leaders of integrity and excellence who will transform Armenian society for the lasting good. That involved calling, character, competence, and community.

Training Centers Ministry of Finance; Armenian Federal Government were needed to involve A Young Adult Business Training Center, "New Life." This can also be a part of a Television Ministry on Avedis TV Yerevan by Dr. Levon Bardakjian. Hospital Visitation at the Medical Centre Yerevan is an important part of gaining the folks trust in Jesus. During this process the vision for Armenia was in process with Eight New FGBMFI Chapters!

ACAPULCO, CUAUTLA AND ATLACAHUALOYA, MEXICO NOVEMBER 15-22, 2010

The vision to unite the churches was birthed from prayer groups led by John Tolo while preparing for the Franklin Graham Crusade in August 2009 for the twin cities areas of Saint Paul and Minneapolis, Minnesota. The key verse for this unity was John 17:3. Bob Bignold, Andres Ariza and Douglas Raine were blessed to be a part of the crusade. FGBMFA relationships were increased during the June 2009 Fire Team Outreach to the twin cities. We encouraged our new friends to continue the outreaches and FGBMFA promised to join John and Andres for future outreaches.

Andres had a burden for the young people in Atlacahualoya. His grandmother, Ninfa Rodriquez, had given Andres property and he saw this property being used for a community center with a focus on Jesus. There would be Internet, Christian music, games, a café ministry. The community center would have an upper room for discipleship. This vision was shared with the Mayor and the Chief of Police. Both John and Andres told God that it was His ministry.

Divine appointments for the November outreach were initiated in Minnesota. By using relationships established during the Graham Crusade, John Tolo and Andres were able to build prayer support to launch our Mexico trip. Catholics and Lutherans were brought together in unity as they prayed together. John obtained many letters of introduction from church and business leaders from the twin cities to take to Atlacahualoya.

Andres' Family and Fire Team
God's Holy Spirit was moving. The town had an estimated six thousand residents and the first man to pray for salvation was Ruben, the Mayor. Carlos Lopez was assigned to be my interpreter and we bonded over the next five days as we met with eighty-seven business owners and employees, of which only three businesses denied prayer.

We prayed blessings for eighty-four business owners and employees. All prayed the sinner's prayer. One business owner refused prayer; however, we praise the Lord that his two employees wanted prayer. One hundred and thirty people on the street prayed to receive Jesus. We ministered to one or two people at a time.

92

We were asked to minister to families in the neighboring town of Axochiapan. A mother of fourteen children requested deliverance from witchcraft and healing for her family. Her oldest son Francisco needed deliverance and wanted to be able to read and understand the Bible. He received deliverance, salvation and the Baptism of the Holy Spirit. After receiving the Holy Spirit, Francisco was able to read and understand John 16. God revealed generational curses and all received deliverance. One couple requested marriage, so we had a wedding.

After one of the team members gave a testimony on forgiveness, reconciliation was experienced. Family members and neighbors were going to each other asking for forgiveness. This was a beautiful picture of God's mercy and grace.

We formed relationships with people on the street, customers in restaurants, church members and business owners. On Thursday evening we ministered to nineteen young men. This was our first FGBMFA dinner meeting. A personal testimony was given and all prayed for salvation, two people received deliverance, and many received the Baptism of the Holy Spirit. When the nineteen young men were asked how many had been in jail, ninety percent raised their hands. Benjamin Moreno volunteered to mentor these men, and Pastor Abel will mentor Ben. Benjamin and Ninfa's home will be used for weekly meetings and discipleship. Ministry continued at our hotel overlooking the Pacific Ocean. People all around us listened as we gave them the message of hope. Many beach vendors responded to God's leading.

CROMWELL, CONNECTICUT 2011

Our teams visited eighty businesses in Cromwell, Connecticut which was the host city for the FGBMFA Southern New England Regional Convention March 24-26, 2011. Twenty five companies were opened to receive prayer, while fifty five companies refused prayer.

FGBMFA New England Leadership members met bi-weekly for prayer lifting up the Fire Teams and the Southern New England Regional Convention. On the weekend of the events God's Holy Spirit manifested God's love in the Cromwell, Connecticut marketplace and the convention. God was glorified as many received salvation, the Baptism of the Holy Spirit and healing.

Comment from Logan Hannington

The Fire team was an experience where I learned to pray for managers and for business owners. This was a mandate that teaches how to possess the land. Also had an encounter with a lady at Burger King and my brother Josiah prayed for her and God healed her knee. I also prayed with a Christian manager at WOW Fitness Center. I learned how to communicate with managers and how to honor them, and be polite even if they denied prayer for them.

Comment from David Tolo A Divine

appointment: One business owner asked the Lord to send a messenger to pray for her and the business. David's team was an answer to prayer.

Comments from John Fay: My team visited nine stores. The owner of "Slice of Heaven" was Hindu. He was open to hear our testimonies and let us pray for his business.

We visited a cigar store and the woman was Catholic. She asked us to pray for her. When I prayed the Lord gave me a word of knowledge for her and tears came to her eyes. She thanked us. Next we visited a doctor's office. The two receptionists wanted us to pray. They bowed their heads while we prayed and they were touched. These two Catholic ladies thanked us for visiting them.

Crystal's Nails was fun for Liz and Paula who were with me. The owner was Hindu and very eager to hear our story. He asked me to pray for him. We also visited an Athletic Club, McDonalds, Super 8 Motel, and even testified with the reception clerks at the Cromwell Hotel too.

Comment from Bill Parsons: On the Thursday before our prayer visits on Friday, we stopped at one business, and the business owner was very respectful but wouldn't let us pray for his employees other than to park in front of the building and say our prayers there. The manager of the business challenged us to go to the business across the street, an Ice Skating School, and to wave to him if that business let us in to pray for them.

We didn't have time to visit the Ice Skating School that day, but the next day Jerry DeFlorio, Josiah Armstrong and Bill Parsons visited the Ice Skating School, and we met with the manager and prayed for there to be peace among the patrons of the school. The Manager even gave us her Christian testimony of how she alone put a huge show dog, whose belly was bloated into a car with what must have been supernatural strength, because it took four men to lift the dog out of the car. We prayed for there to be peace and harmony and good conduct by the patrons of the ice skating rink.

APRIL – MAY 2011
FIRE TEAM OUTREACHES TO THE REPUBLIC OF GEORGIA AND ARMENIA

Our team of Douglas Raine, John Schmook and Dr. Jesse Cradduck were blessed with opportunities to impact lives in the nations of Georgia and Armenia. Our national coordinators Hovhannes Tovmasyan (Armenia) and Aleks Kvinikadze (Georgia) did an excellent job scheduling business meetings, university appointments, church services, special meetings, and seminars.

The business seminars opened many doors to share our testimonies. Current Government and Orthodox Church politics have restricted marketplace evangelism and inhibited business

startups and expansions. The people
were hungry for business opportunities and were
very receptive to the message of hope.

Almost every meeting resulted in salvations, while
many received the Baptism of the Holy Spirit,
prophecy and prayers for healings which resulted
in expressions of thanksgiving. We appreciated
Pastors opening their pulpits for us to minister.
The Holy Spirit moved in every service, and the
enthusiasm of the local Joshua generation was
incredible for both them and us.

Our message of depending on God and seeking His
direction in life was understood by many and
embraced by the young adults and youth. Pastors
were open to our methods of evangelism in the
marketplace using our testimonies. Invitations
were extended to join FGBMFA and we found
several candidates to start new chapters.

Many students said that they would like to
translate teachings from the training website into
their language. We found a lot of raw talent that
was ready to step-up to the plate and swing for the
fences. Many businessmen and students promised
to send me their testimonies for posting on the

website. Listed below is a sampling of divine appointments in the marketplace:

Vanadzor, Armenia

Our first meeting was scheduled with eighteen men and two women. Several received salvation and the Spirit Baptism. Vanik gathered people on the street and brought them to a classroom to receive Jesus. We were then invited by a professor at an engineering university to describe how to solve internal corrosion to students.

So many people were touched by God. Bankers heard the Gospel there, and TV and radio programming spread the Word. We met with a military motor pool training class who heard the Gospel for the first time.

Gyumri, Armenia

We participated in an Easter Service by sharing testimonies and serving communion. An incredible children's program followed the service, where both orphans and children of church members ranging from seven to fourteen years of age, recited scripture, performed drama skits, presented the Resurrection with great acting, dancing and musical talent. We were given a DVD of the performance.

A business meeting followed after the service. Hamlet, a dentist told his story as did Ara. Hamlet is the local FGBMFI chapter president which was started last year after our meeting. Everyone gave a brief business background, and they have the vision for evangelism and discipleship.

All in all we presented the Gospel in church services to an estimated three thousand one hundred people. In the Business Seminars, attendance at Tbilisi, Georgia, Vanadzor, Armenia, Gyumri, Armenia, and Yerevan, Armenia four hundred and one people heard the Word. Individual Marketplace contacts were twenty-six people, so the total contacts hearing the Gospel was three thousand nine hundred and twenty-eight.

KURDISTAN: OCTOBER 16-31, 2011
Outreach to Kurdistan

The Kurds occupy an area of Turkey with twenty million people, and in Iraq they have five million people. Iran had ten million people, and Syria and Russia one and a half million. The area that they occupy is rich in oil. The Kurds are descendants of the Medes.

On October 18, 2011, Fire Team Members Gene Arnold and Douglas Raine met with Kurdish President Dr. Kamal Kirkuki, and Parliament Members Zakia Seeid and Shireen Fattah, and we received favor in all of Kurdistan. While there Gene Arnold was rushed to Azadi Teaching General Hospital Duhok which lasted three days in critical condition. The emergency room was exceptional as Mohammed Tawfig Bawarri took us from doctor to doctor. and I asked the Lord how will this glorify You? Mohammed had his two sons come and rotate to be with Gene when we went to eat or bathroom breaks. This was truly an act of kindness and greatly appreciated. Gene was miraculously healed.

Meeting The Leaders Of Nations

In November 2011 we were in northern Iraq meeting with the USA Ambassador and military team. Our military would be pulling out, and they were very concerned for the safety of Christians. Many Christians were leaving Baghdad and Mosul and seeking safety in Kurdistan. We also met with the Catholic leadership, evangelical Pastors and congregations, the President of Kurdistan along with several members of congress; we had favor with everyone! Divine appointments were setup with businessmen, faculty and students in universities.

Then something unexpected happened when my team member got sick. We checked him into the Duhok Hospital where the doctors and staff were very helpful and professional. As I prayed for his health, the Holy Spirit said, "Go pray for that man across the aisle." I took my interpreter and asked what was wrong and he said, "I am having severe chest pains and I am scheduled for heart surgery this afternoon." He granted me permission to pray in Jesus' name. When I finished praying he said, "Your Jesus healed me." Thank you Jesus.

I then returned to pray for my friend and he was getting worse. Three hours later friends of the man whose heart was healed, came over to me and took me to hospital rooms to pray for patients. When I returned to my friend, he was healed too. We checked out of the hospital. I have no idea how many people were healed by God that day, but the glory of God was everywhere.

BEMIDJI / LEECH INDIAN RESERVATION – OJIBWE TRIBE

Outreaches in Minnesota - February 1-5, 2012
The Koinonia team had been in prayer for several months calling out to God to intervene and protect young Native American girls from being sold into sex trafficking. God was answering their prayers as many gang leaders were being busted in a sting operation in Saint Paul. Both Karen and Cindy who were counselors to the tribe shared horrifying stories. Our leadership team met with Tribal Leader Eli Hunt, a righteous man, to pray for God's wisdom and protection.

Saturday February 4, 2012
We had a joint breakfast meeting at the Electric Company with FGBMF and Aglow International Bemidji Chapters. Douglas Raine emceed, and over one hundred and twenty attended. Evangelical leaders attended and the theme was to take back the city. The atmosphere was spiritually charged.

Later that week I was on my way to breakfast when a young adult reached out and grabbed me and said, "You have a word for me!" I said, "Jesus loves you." With that the demons began to manifest in him and blasphemed God. This response caught me by surprise, but the demons were cast out, and I walked away. He ran after me and was crying, "I want to receive Jesus, I want to receive Jesus." I turned around and he prayed to receive Jesus. We embraced and praised Jesus.

Sunday February 5
Team leaders brought the morning message at three area churches and the entire team provided spiritual support. Salvations, baptisms and healings were experienced by the congregations. Relationships were being built all over the community.

OUTREACHES IN GEORGIA AND TEXAS
2012 Stone Mountain, Georgia
FGBMFA Teams gathered at Stone Mountain on July 4, 2012. Teams were instructed to gather families together and take their photo with our smart phones. While taking pictures, we would share our testimony and close with an altar call. Several times I would have a family member translate from English to Spanish. The largest family gathering was 25 people.

Hunt County Fair Texas

For twenty consecutive years we would share "The

Two Question Test" at the Hunt County Fair. There was one young man in 2012 that heard the plan of salvation. When asked if he would like to pray to receive Jesus, he said not now because I have a lot of living to do. That evening he was hit by a pickup truck on FM 1570 in front of the Fairgrounds and killed. We were all saddened, but his story brought many to the booth to receive Jesus Christ as Savior.

Dallas Texas Christmas Gift 2012

The Saturday before Christmas Operation Care International invites the homeless and people living in the projects to a Christmas Party at the Dallas Convention Center. Evangelism teams are stationed in one section to minister to the single adults, and the other section ministers to families. Between three hundred and five hundred volunteers lead guest in the "Plan of Salvation" using a survey. Information is collected on our guests for follow-up. There is a special location called HELPS in each evangelism area which ministers deliverance and the baptism of the Holy Spirit.

Attendance ranged from 8,000 to 18,000 people. Guests then go into the large ministry area to have their feet washed, medical, dental, and eye exams, receive sleeping bags, clothes, gifts, a hot meal, and listen to choirs.

All of these mission trips by Douglas Raine were a part of many others, For instance, there were two trips to Panama where one time one of the team took a microphone at the beginning of a soccer game, and shared his testimony. When he was done, four hundred people stood and prayed to receive Jesus.

There were five trips to the United Arab Emirates after which five Chapters of FGBMFI had been established. Over the years were many mission trips made by Douglas. To wit:
2 Outreaches to Nigeria, 10 to Armenia and 4 to the Republic of Georgia, 2 to Taiwan, 1 to Hong Kong, 1 to Singapore, 1 to Honduras, 15 to Mexico, 1 to Malaysia, 1 to Japan, 7 to UK, 3 to Ireland, 3 to Germany, 4 to Ukraine and started 4 churches, 1 to Russia, 1 to Most of Europe,
3 Israel, 2 Turkey, 1 to Bulgaria, 5 to Minnesota, 3 to Montana, 20 to Texas, 4 to Louisiana, 2 to Tennessee, 4 to Oklahoma, 2 to Kansas,
2 to Missouri, 1 to Colorado, 2 to Maryland, 4 to New York, 2 to Connecticut, 4 to Florida, 4 to Georgia, 2 to Arkansas, and 2 to New Mexico.

I would travel with Bob Bignold to start chapters in USA, Asia and Africa

Richard L. McBain

Section Two
Testimonies of Gary Vanover
Ministry A Blessing 2 Nations (B2N)
Ministry In Panama

Betty Moodie and her husband Ellio and Betty's sister Nina have done an excellent job with our B2N ministry in Panama. In April of 2000 Betty felt it was time we started a new work in three separate areas. Rio West, Tres Mile and an area called Un Mile, these are the Spanish names of the closest villages to Betty's village.

We walked into the jungle where Betty's children would regularly show up on Saturday mornings for games and simple Bible stories. B2N took the simple concept of teaching children how to read and write by using Scriptures. This is how the early American pioneers did it when they headed out west. If the early settlers could do it then why not duplicate the same procedure in the jungles of Panama.

On that April day, Betty shared that the only decent place to meet and teach was the exact same spot where the witches met regularly to do their nightly incantations. Joslin was one the young boys of that first group of young children. We continued working with this group of children and we assigned an adult to cover these youth's in prayer and to give them encouragement and direction in their lives.

Many of these children come to our Bible study and game day as they enjoy being loved and a part of something exciting. Many of these youth come from alcoholic homes and desperately need this outreach provided by B2N through your financial support. Also Betty and our Panama team prayerfully want to start more AWANA clubs in areas that are unreached with the gospel. Our B2N team continues to impact these communities by regularly taking food and clothing. During Christmas the team from B2N takes gifts to the least of these.

Fredrick Yaro In Ghana

Fredrick Yaro and I met as I was walking up the steps of the church in Kumasi, Ghana. His eyes fixed on mine the same as it must have been with Peter and John at the front of the temple at the Gate Beautiful with the lame man. It was a God encounter, and it seemed this young man's eyes were saying, "Pastor, can you be the one to help me break this demonic stronghold over my life?"

At that very moment It was as though I knew exactly how to pray! When I finished the prayer I knew that our God had intervened in his life and began to heal him from the things that had tormented him, and it was a visible breakthrough for Fredrick Yaro.

Rev. Fredrick Yaro, now leads our B2N work on the ground in Ghana as he perseveres to establish churches in many unreached areas. We at B2N believe in putting real people in the field who have a testimony that can be the hands and arms and voice for our Lord. Here is a story recently sent out by Fredrick Yaro about a young man that he knows he is to disciple.

Fredrick led Otto, a young Muslim man to the Lord in his village. Otto was told by his parents either convert back to Islam or they can't let him come home and they will no longer pay for his university expenses. An urgent prayer was sent out to our staff and team in the U.S, Guatemala, Panama, Costa Rica and Zambia. The next day after much prayer Fredrick sent out this praise report and Otto continues to give this testimony to the glory of God. Otto's parents relented and changed their minds and their decision. God had answered our prayer. Otto is now allowed to move back in his parent's home and they will continue to provide for his education. Most importantly Otto is allowed to continue to walk as a Christian and he will absolutely worship God. He continues to be mentored by Fredrick Yaro:

Jose In Guatemala

We had gone to see a young man named Jose (not his real name) who had a desire to leave the gang life behind. Jose had witnessed his best friend being killed in the streets of Guatemala, presumably by other gang members. He had gone on a long, drug binge and was fearfully on the edge! Before Jose's friend died, he had been doing everything to convince him to accept Jesus as he himself had only recently become saved.

Jose was very close to receiving Jesus when his friend was gunned down. I stepped in at the right time but I knew it was his friend who had planted all the seeds for salvation to take root. Jose received Jesus that night but could not get free of all the drugs that was in his system. I explained that God is a jealous God, but He does want to forgive us when we repent of our sins.

We knew that the devil does not want to let go of someone who has been doing his work, so we taught Jose for an hour or so and we reminded the enemy that he has no legal ground to harass this young man anymore. We reminded the devil that this young man was under the blood covenant of Jesus and legally his drug addiction was also under the blood covenant. This young man only had to be convinced that not only was he worthy of Jesus dying on the cross for his sins but that he could also receive eternal life and receive life more abundantly because of the cross.

When Jose walked into church that night, many young kids who were emulating him also walked into church as we began to see the breaking of this vicious cycle in Jose's life? A month later he was killed by a rival gang as he was returning from visiting his mother. As tragic as it was for those who loved him, we knew where he and his friend were spending eternity; in Heaven with Jesus!

Gustavo In Barcenous

My eyes met with a stranger's on the streets of Barcenous, and I lifted up a prayer that I wanted an opportunity to talk to this man about Jesus. My team had other places where they wanted me to go first and pray or talk to certain people. Near the end of the day, we went to a house where a man had requested a visit. I recognized him immeddiately as the man with whom our eyes had locked earlier that day.

I knew this was a prearranged meeting by God himself. I always ask for divine appointments and this one had the finger of God written all over it. I prayed for discernment to be able to step into this man's life with the exact precision of the Holy Spirit. I noticed he had washed his hair and cleaned up for this prearranged meeting. Instantly, I knew what to tell him, that God wanted him to come to Him just as he was, and that God would do the rest of the "cleaning-up process".

I then asked if he had a drinking problem and he said that he did. In his mind, he could not come to Jesus unclean just as he would not meet a man of God in his house without getting clean first.

Gustavo received Jesus and later that night went to church as a born again believer. He now works with our youth in that mountain church.

First Church Plant By B2N In Ghana

I accepted an invitation to preach in Ghana, West Africa. Our plan was to visit a village and ask for permission to return in the evening to share the gospel. The villages are part of a Muslim culture; and women in leadership are often frowned upon. We arrived at the village with our translator, eager to be introduced to the Chief.

Charlene, my wife was so excited; she couldn't wait until the evening to share her faith. She plunged into telling the Chief about the Bible and because of sin, their need for a Savior. All around the Chief stood his council, about ten to fifteen strong African warriors, their eyes showing no fear but rather an intense commitment to protect their Chief.

Suddenly, I realized what we were doing. Here was a remote village in Africa with a woman telling the Chief he was a sinner and needed salvation. Was she breaking protocol by speaking

115

directly to the Chief? Was she insulting him by telling him that he needed salvation for his sins?

The Chief slowly nodded his head with acceptance. He was very old and frail, but he took my hand and allowed me to pray for him. We prayed a prayer of repentance, and I asked his permission to address his council. He agreed. The tribal leaders listened as I explained again the gospel. They, too, prayed to receive Jesus. We spent a wonderful time with the Manprulia people. The children even had their first taste of chocolate! With great admiration, we watched the villagers sway to the beat of homemade drums and other musical instruments.

As we prepared to leave, our translator approached us with amusement on his face. He carried in his hand three guinea fowl hens, a bowl of peanuts, and six guinea fowl eggs. He shyly told me the chief was inviting Charlene to become one of his many wives! These gifts of food of this quality was a great sacrifice, and were a pledge of his matrimonial intentions. It was a show of great respect. I declined his offer to marry Charlene, declaring that she was my bride!

We humbly asked the Chief for a gift of ten acres of land to build a small church on. The Chief agreed and the men of the village brought homemade tools to mark the property and clear the land for the church. While the men were clearing Savannah Grass away, a villager rushed in and shouted, "You must build the church quickly so the blind can see! You must build the church quickly so the blind can see!" Later in the day, Charlene prayed for the Chief who was losing his sight because of cataracts. She watched in amazement as his "watering eyes" changed to clear brown eyes.

A Blessing to the Nations did indeed build a church there in that village. Months later a group of Christians that we were connected with went and visited the church. In that first service that was preached by our friends, who were then just ordinary businessmen, the first person they prayed for was blind. God healed him and restored his sight. That businessman is now in fulltime ministry as he saw the hand of God move mightily. When I had heard the villager say to build the church quickly, I thought it was for evangelism purposes. Yes, that also, but God wanted to show He honors obedience because we did build the church quickly and the blind did see. Dr. Jesus still heals.

Every Sunday the church is full to capacity with 200-300 people praising their God and lifting up the name of Jesus. On that campaign, the majority of the people in the Village of Buggia that were practicing voodoo, switched and became born-again Christians through the effort of some simple questions in the Word of God. Before we left, they asked if they could change the name of the village to either my name or the name of our ministry. I suggested that they change the name from Buggia, the voodoo power-town of West Africa, to the name of Jesus power-town!

A Call to Ministry, Part I: Guatemala

A pastor friend of mine suggested I watch a video by the Sentinel Group and well-known Christian author George Otis Junior on the transformation of cities around the world through the power of prayer. After watching this video, I was offered a chance to be an attendee in a great Christian conference being held in Guatemala. While the conference was the main reason for our going down, Charlene and I boldly told others that we were actually going to find the Pastor featured in the video and find out more about the amazing transformation of the Miracle City of Almolonga, Guatemala.

Many of our Christian friends asked if we were planning on sightseeing or deep sea fishing. Our response confused many of them as we said we were going down for the "Transformation Anointing" that we saw take place in the video. In the village, prior to the prayer answered by God, there had been much corruption. Alcoholism was prevalent, rare forms of cancer attacked even the very young, and a large portion of the villagers worshipped a god by the name of Mashmon. Almolonga was a very poor village, even by Latin American standards, as the few crops only went to harvest every 60 days.

After many years of prayer, the village encountered a revival through the incredible outpouring of God's favor. The only four jails in town closed as there was no longer a need for them. Alcoholism was virtually eliminated, the rare forms of cancer stopped, and the majority of bars became churches.

To show their appreciation to God, they started naming their businesses after some of the names of God to honor Him. However, the most amazing aspect of God's favor was the ability of the land to go from 60 days, which is the normal harvest time, to even lower than 40 days. As the outpouring of God's favor continued, it dropped to the present low of 24 days that a new crop of vegetables could go to market! On hearing these results, I was even more interested in visiting this city and meeting the Pastors who ushered in God's outpouring, Pastor Mariano Reskeche and his wife Miquela.

Before leaving for Guatemala, we had contacted a young 16-year old Guatemalan girl whom we had hosted for a weekend trip to Atlanta. She suggest= ed that we come to dinner the first night after the conference because her parents wanted to thank us for taking such good care of their daughter while in America. We were waiting in their home that night and were informed that another couple was also coming.

Soon the doorbell rang, and to my surprise, in walked the Pastors from the video, Pastor Mariano and his wife Miquela. He looked at me and with confidence knew that I wanted to ask him something. I explained I was interested in the transformation anointing, and was it feasible to pray for me so we could start walking in Divine revelation. He suggested that I drive to his hometown and have lunch and then he would pray for me.

Before we left that night, Charlene realized that the 16-year-old's grandmother was part of the prayer team that helped rebirth the revival, and she was also there that night. Many prayers were prayed over us as we still had not received the official call from God for full-time ministry. When the intercessors prayed for us, Charlene and I both had great confidence that this was one of the final missing keys, and this would propel us into full-time ministry.

A few days later, Pastor Mariano did pray for us at his church in Almolonga where the city had been transformed by the power of God through prayer. After they laid hands on us in prayer, I didn't feel really different, but somehow we both knew that this was just the beginning of our new life as we now understood the Divine connection, which had just jumpstarted our new destiny.

Richard L. McBain

Bosnian Refugees

One day Charlene read a story in the newspaper about Bosnian POW's. The article stated that the enemies of the Bosnians boasted that they would indeed follow the Dayton Peace Accord agreement and release the prisoners daily; however, they would shoot them as they left the camps if they would not get on planes to go to foreign countries other than their own countries. The article explained that the Serbian Croatians were unwilling to allow these prisoners to return to their own countries and to their armies to fight again.

Charlene was moved with compassion, and dramatically declared, "Oh, if that happened to my husband, I would want someone to help him." The only way the Serbo-Croatians would allow the prisoners to be released, would be for some country to take them in and let them live there. "I would help these Bosnians if only I knew how," she thought. She had no idea how quickly God would challenge her to live up to her words.

Within two days, the organization called World Relief had contacted me, as I was heading up the missions program in a local church. World Relief

122

helps people in war-torn areas of the world to relocate. We had worked with them when the church became involved in sponsoring several Bosnian families. World Relief told us about six men, all related, who needed official sponsorship. Apparently, World Relief would receive the men as they left the camps, whisk them away to a plane, and fly them to safety. However, they needed someone willing to receive them on the other end and be responsible for them, helping them to get settled with shelter and jobs and caring for all their needs until they became assimilated. Oh, by the way, did I mention that they would be here the next day!

When I discussed this with Charlene, she had a shocked look on her face. Had God heard her "boastful" words ? She took a deep breath, humbled herself, and then said, "They all can come to my house." We did not know how we would manage, but we knew God was in charge and He would provide. We had a lot of Christian friends who gave us a hard time because we were accepting six Muslims (although, later, we learned that they were ethnic Muslims, not practicing Muslims).

A short time later, I walked into the house with six frightened, emaciated men for us to take care of. That's when the miracles began! The men had paperwork from World Relief stating what the name of their village was, the names of their families, and even telephone numbers for their families. However, the village had been ravaged and families displaced and many of the telephones were for distant relatives. They were not even confident they were working phone numbers. Much of this information was obsolete as the war had destroyed the village, torn down her power and phone lines, and all the families were evacuated.

As Charlene made them breakfast the first day, she showed them eggs to see if they would like to have them. She realized that while they were starved, they longed even more to know if their families were alive. She had them use our telephone to try to call their family numbers in Bosnia or their distant relatives' phone numbers. Over and over, they dialed the numbers with no success because the calls would not go through.

Charlene saw the anguish on their faces, and she pictured phone lines down destroyed by bombs.

Then she saw her Bible lying on the counter. She knew the men were ethnic Muslims, but she wanted to communicate to them the need to pray and ask God to connect the phone lines and put their calls through. She found the word "God" in her Bible and showed them. The youngest, Emir, who was 16 years old at the time, said "Oh, yes, Mog," their word for God.

They did not understand prayer but removed their hats and stood respectfully while Charlene prayed. They again dialed the numbers, and someone answered! It was Emir's mother, and his father Emin was standing there in anticipation. Soon everyone was shouting with joy, "Yes, we are all alive, but we are in America and cannot walk home!"

We realized in so many ways that God was with us during our times with the Bosnians. Several of our Bosnian friends got jobs at popular restaurants. One of them was Steak and Shake, and Gary would set his alarm for 2:00 a.m. every morning, get up, go to Steak and Shake to pick them up and bring them home. Eventually, we found an apartment available in Lawrenceville where other Bosnian refugees lived. We got donations for furniture and set them up to live in their own apartment.

One day, one of them got a job at McDonald's. He needed a bicycle to ride to and from work so that he could get to his second job on time. On our way to work that morning, Charlene and I talked about the "need of the day." It was a bicycle, a dependable bicycle. By 1:00 p.m. that day, one of my customers came into the barbershop with a very nice bicycle. He had restored it and then decided he wanted a new one. "Could you use a bicycle in any of the good projects that you are doing, Gary?" God knows our needs before we even ask!

A few days later, a power bill arrived in the mail for the Bosnians' apartment. The amount of the bill was $98.17. I now smiled as another customer stuck his head in the door of the barbershop with a $100 bill and humbly said, "I thought maybe you could use this money for your refugees." The Bible promises us that God will supply all your needs according to His riches in glory!

The Bosnians became our close friends. We often visited them daily, or at least weekly. They became accustomed to our prayers for their needs, and they trusted us and "our" God to meet their every need.

One day, one of them shared with us his desire to return to Bosnia for a visit. Charlene knew they didn't know Jesus and His great love for them. It was time for us to testify to them of Jesus' love and sacrifice on the cross, but it would be necessary to have a really good translator. We prayed and scheduled dinner for them in our home; and then looked with excited anticipation for a translator. We thought perhaps a diplomat from Bosnia would call or a college professor of the language, but these things did not happen as the time approached.

Charlene became concerned. "I know God has heard my request for a translator to share the gospel with my friends! Why doesn't He answer?" I meekly suggested Dario, a ten-year old Bosnian child we occasionally used to translate. We called Dario and invited him to have dinner and translate for us. Charlene gave the plan of salvation in a very simple way because Dario couldn't translate big words. When she asked the Bosnian men if they would like to invite Jesus into their hearts, Dario interrupted her with a question,

Richard L. McBain

"Please, Miss Charlene, I want to ask Jesus to come and live in my heart also; am I old enough to pray this prayer?" With humbleness and great joy, Charlene replied, "Tonight you did a man's job translating for me; tonight you will ask Jesus into your heart as a man, and He will receive you as a man."

Dario and his family moved to Ohio a week later and we never saw them again; but we know that God can be trusted and He has them in His hand.

Junior

Little five-year old Junior had seen his mother, Lauda, rise from her sick bed just two months earlier. He now witnessed another miracle as the B2N team walked out the door and started down the next street. Junior ran ahead of us, and as a baseball player, literally slid up to the next door. Do you understand that this five-year old *knew* that another victory was coming? He had been with us at all 27 houses that day. He began shouting, "The brothers are coming, the brothers are coming to tell you about Jesus! Open the door quickly!"

The people came rushing and asked, "Does your

God heal water on the brain?" Apparently Jesus does, because that day he healed a lady who was suffering from convulsions. Also, those that were in bondage to alcohol and drugs became radically free. Many were released from generational curses of their ancestors. They then could easily receive the Baptism of the Holy Spirit after confessing Jesus as their Lord and Saviour!

On a recent, unannounced visit to Junior's village, as we walked through the village, Junior saw me and my team. He ran home to clean up, and then walked with us, because he now knew that Jesus is looking for anyone to use who has the faith to be used.

The Village of Barcenous where I Flipped Another Witch

Lauda was confined to lying in bed with a serious back injury. We had just led a gang leader Jose to the Lord and walked him through a demonic deliverance of a drug stronghold. (Unfortunately, he was violently murdered on April 4th, three weeks after we had led him to the Lord, because he renounced his gang membership.) My team and I were on our way to church knowing God had

129

showed up. I was excited, so I said a dart prayer, "Lord, give me one more house." A seven-year old girl came running out and said, "My mama needs a healing, please do not pass us by!"

There was already talk of a gringo in their midst who was laying hands on sick people and they were being healed. Lauda was a practicing witch and thought that it was absurd that we believe we have power from God. She felt she was the most educated and highly spiritual person in the village and yet, she needed a healing.

While she believed there was a God, surely, He did not need to use someone to walk in and pray for her. She told God that these Christians mean well, but really, to heal people using the name of Jesus only is absurd! She turned her face to the wall and was pleased that her husband had more sense than to call for those praying Christians as they walked by, but her daughter had the faith to not let this opportunity pass by. Lauda was healed when my team and I laid hands on her. The Holy Spirit went to the exact spot that needed healing. She slowly got out of bed but her eyes said that she was healed by The Blood of Jesus. That night Lauda walked into church, and before the night was over, was jumping for joy. When her husband saw her dancing, he then asked us to tell him about this Jesus who still heals.

Lauda Walks Away from her Healing

Lauda asked if ABTTN would return to her village as the entire village was waiting for more miracles. **Mark 16:20** says, "…signs and wonders have to follow when the gospel is preached." She volunteered to host us for lunch and dinner, and a group of zealous youth, ages 15-17, offered to escort the ABTTN around to a group of homes that needed Jesus or deliverance or healing. As it turned out, the young man leading the group had lived in another village and I had done some "tweaking on him for deliverance. (Tweaking just sounds better) Lauda ran to the first house to tell them that we were in town. In this house a young man needed a miracle on one of his legs which was noticeably shorter than the other.

When I entered the boy's home, he wasn't there, but ten other people were there waiting for prayer. All of them received Jesus as we shared the word of God and took them down "Romans Road".

Romans 3:10, 23; 6:23; 5:8. I told the boy's
mother, "Stay here and expect that healing."
Jesus wants to honor your faith and obedience.
When I returned, even more people were waiting
to hear the word and receive prayer.

The gospel was presented again, and more people
received Jesus including the young man, Brian,
whom we were to pray for. Even as I prayed, his
leg instantly became the same length as the other.
Brian's leg grew out! I heard it and saw it move
two inches. He then walked normally. The mother,
the children, and the boy all began to cry and
praise God, as they saw the boy being healed!
Most in attendance showed up for church that
night, and I preached the shortest message ever.
All I said was, "Today your Jesus visited your
village. He still heals and saves people."

They worshipped Jesus and danced for an hour. On
a sad note, because Lauda lost her stature in the
village, she soon went back to witchcraft, and her
back problem returned. She also talked the young
man, Brian, into believing his healing was a
fake. Soon, his leg shifted back and he was
limping again. My word of encouragement is to
stay in faith. It is harder to keep your miracle than

to receive your miracle.

Flipped Another Witch

I had prayed for a young man at the altar and he was slain in the Spirit. When the service ended, the Pastor said there was a problem and that the young man could not get up. They used the word "paralyzed." While I walked across the room, the devil whispered in my mind, "That is it! Now you will be sued, and your ministry will be closed in disgrace." I know this voice, and I responded by going over, reaching down, slapping the young man on the knee, and then snatching him up. He landed on his feet confused and dazed, but okay. I could not give a reason for anything, but said I would be in prayer and consult my prayer team.

The next night, the young man returned with a friend and said he could only speak with me and no one else should hear him. This was a mountain area where he had done Spiritual Mapping and determined that there were 50+ witches in this village. (Spiritual Mapping is to an evangelist what an X-ray is to a doctor.) Apparently when he had gotten home that night, his kitchen chairs had danced around the table all by themselves. He was on his way to have himself committed to an institution and stopped by where I was preaching and asked for my advice on this issue.

I shouted, "Thank you, Jesus!" as now I knew that his destiny was so large that the enemy was trying to stop him. I gave him my anointing oil and told him to anoint the back door first and then go and open the front door and make everything that is not of God leave.

The next night, he returned and said it worked! One minor detail that he left out, however, was that his mother was the number one witch in that area. Upon her return to the house, she said, "What have you done here? There is no more power in this house." Months later this lady came and asked me to take her through deliverance. She got free and is still free. She is now our top prayer warrior for A Blessing To The Nations. She saw the manifest presence of the power of the Holy Spirit.

Rufina In Jungles Of Panama

On my last trip into the jungles of Panama, we visited all six of our AWANA programs. AWANA is our Bible memorization program that has been ongoing for the last six years.

We had completed our teaching when an older man sitting in the back of the group asked to see me. Apparently his daughter was in a coma and he asked me. "Does my God still heal?" I knew he was not wanting to discuss my theological view but that he was in serious need for prayer for his daughter. I agreed to go with him to his hut. My past experience in these villages has allowed me to see a strong presence of witch doctors or Brujos.

I suspected this girl had had a curse put on her by a close relative. As soon as I started praying over Rufina, she came out of the coma. She was dazed, confused, and dehydrated. She confirmed my suspicions that her ex- boyfriend had been to visit the witch doctor to buy a curse on Rufina's life. When Rufina was alert enough, we made sure that she had received Jesus as her Lord and savior. Eventually all her family have now embraced Christianity. Rufina has made a full recovery.

MS - 13

Mara Salvatruca MS – 13 is an international criminal group that originated in Los Angeles in the 70s and 80s. I first encountered them when I was traveling El Salvador as they are predominantly out of that country. The MS stands for Mara

Salvatruca. Mara means gang and Salva Salvador and Trucha which translates roughly into being street-smart.

They refer to themselves as a gang who likes to rape kill and control. I had been a regular speaker in a drug / gang program in Guatemala for Nikki Cruz and their work with gang members. I had been preaching regularly to a pastor in downtown Guatemala City and he suggested I come out and work with his gang program that did include MS 13s.

On the day I arrived to do a simple Bible study I was immediately aware of the fact that the majority of the people in this halfway house are part of the MS 13 gang lifestyle. The young pastor was doing a great job getting these guys off the street, and cleaned up a little bit, at least enough to be able sit through a Bible study while at the same time to be free of the stronghold of crack cocaine.

Gathered in a small room were at least 10 to 15 MS 13 gang members. I had been aware of their atrocities, but I was also aware of the fact most of these men wanted to lead a somewhat normal life.

136

Normally when these guys leave that gang style of MS 13 they are executed. This was in a remote area of Guatemala and the MS 13 really didn't have a stronghold in that area like in El Salvador.

As I was teaching a very simple basic Bible study I was nudged by the Holy Spirit to do something I had never done before. All of the men love to walk around bare chested showing off their massive MS 13 tattoos and the brutality of the lifestyle they had been in. The Holy Spirit had me ask the men if I could anoint their tattoos and cancel the evil that had gone with the purpose of those tattoos.

It seemed like a normal request and at the time I had no idea what was about to happen. As prompted by the Holy Spirit I rubbed each one down with anointing oil and at the same time I canceled the evil that was intended to go with each one of those gruesome tattoos. Instantly as I started to rub the tattoos and call those things null and void each one of those men were absolutely knocked out by the Holy Ghost. The ironic thing was that the men fell absolutely as if they had been shot, many laying against each other, some laying in a chair sideways, but every one of them was completely out cold and I believe God was answering those prayers of the men who wanted to come out of that crazy gang lifestyle.

Of course the tattoos were still there but I believe God was honoring their request to grow closer to the heart of Jesus. I followed up with the halfway house before I left Guatemala on that trip, and was pleasantly surprised that a couple of the men were already doing street preaching having come into their destiny because they had been touched by the hand of God.

Our Testimony & The Blood Of The Lamb

Section Three
Testimonies of
Richard "Dick" McBain

My Mother saw to it that I knew the Lord in a real way from as long as I can remember. I was raised a Catholic and had a close relationship with Jesus. I would come home from school and many times go to my room to look out of my upstairs back window and talk to the Lord. God gave me many miracles in my life, and I want to share them with you.

Miracles In The Vietnam War

I was assigned to the 101st Airborne Division in Vietnam after being drafted out of college. I was combat infantry and lived in the jungle for almost a year. On May 7, 1970 we made a combat assault by helicopter into a jungle covered mountain with a Regiment of NVA (North Vietnam Army) dug way into the mountain.

We had men killed that first day and some wounded. The battle raged at different times night and day, and the mountain was blasted with artillery, huge guns from the warships in the Gulf

140

of Tonkin, Cobra Gunships, and F-4 Phantom jets with high explosive bombs and napalm. After each of our lambasting the mountain, a platoon would move up to recon and would walk into many enemy soldiers who had been unscathed weathering the attacks in the shelter of the mountain.

On the third day, after more bombing and napalm strikes, our CO (Commanding Officer) called Lieutenant Richardson, an Airborne Ranger and our Platoon Leader, and told him to take three others with him to recon the area of the Napalm strike. I was selected with two others, and the three of us reluctantly moved out to our destination. Smitty, a former Hell's Angel in the US walked point, followed by the Lieutenant, then Sgt. Tom Brennan, and lastly me with the radio and rifle.

The enemy let Smitty cross the burned-out clearing and into the jungle on the other side of the smoldering Napalm. Suddenly an enemy machine gun opened up and we heard Smitty scream. The Lieutenant ran across the clearing, and Tom followed. I was the only one left in the burning opening and trying to watch behind us. I heard an explosion and the Lieutenant yelled at me to bring

141

the radio to him. He was bleeding above his eye from the grenade thrown at him.

I started to receive a lot of enemy rifle fire at me and saw that we had been surrounded. Bullets were hitting all around me but not hitting me. The CO was calling on the radio to see what was happening and I was too busy firing to answer his calls. I began to cry just waiting for bullets to hit me, and cried out to the Lord, "Lord please get me out of this and I'll be your man, please Lord!"

I began to move forward firing with all I had while answering the CO on the radio. I said in a panic "Sir you've got to get to us; need immediate assistance; LT and Smitty have been hit, over." He answered, "Now settle down son, we are trying to get through to you but you are completely surrounded. You have to hold on; hold on, out."

As I reached the jungle on the other side of the smoldering Napalm I heard an explosion up in front of me. When I crawled through the thick jungle I saw Lieutenant Richardson with his arm blown off from a satchel charge thrown at him. I was firing as fast as I could, and looked over seeing Tom coming running back up to me through the clearing. He had run down to see if he could help get the guys through to us be he couldn't.

I crawled out in front of the Lieutenant shooting at everyone in sight until I burned my M-16 up; the barrel was white-hot. The enemy threw a grenade at me but I threw it back. Next they threw a satchel charge at me and it landed just out of my reach. I buckled as it exploded throwing me into the air. As I hit the ground near the Lieutenant I check to see if I had my arms and my legs, and I did. I reached over and took the Lieutenant's weapon which he could no longer fire and again started shooting up the area.

Just when Tom and I thought we were dead, I heard an American M-60 Machine gun commin up behind us. I looked and saw Mark Bogio with the gun under his arm and belts of ammo over his other forearm shooting everything, The other guys broke through with him, with the medic looking at the Lieutenant who had also been shot in the neck when he tried to get up next to me. Mark looked at us and said, "You guys get out of here; we got this!" He didn't have to tell me twice.

As I crawled down the ridgeline and got to the

smoldering Napalm area I saw Smitty bleeding out of the top of his head. When he was shot he dove off the side of the ridgeline and crawled down behind us. I put my dressing on his wound and called for the medic. We were still under fire so as the medic got to Smitty, I crawled out in front of them to keep the enemy from shooting them. Doc looked at me and said, "LT is dead Dick!" I was quiet for a few seconds but then said to him, "Well we got to get Smitty back to the LZ for Medevac or he's next."

There were now about eight or so of us heading down the trail, and I had Smitty's arm over my shoulder walking him with me. We didn't know that we had been resurrounded, and as I got to a large tree enemy soldiers opened up on me and Smitty, shooting the bark off the tree next to us. I dropped Smitty to the ground and turned and fired on automatic at the direction the firing was coming from. It stopped and I assumed I had sent them to meet God.

We then had a firefight with the enemy surrounding us and finally either killed them or they ran, I don't know which. You can't see in triple canopy jungle! We finally got to the LZ and

Smitty, Tom and I were Medevac'd. As the chopper left the mountain we had too many wounded on it and it fell from the sky. The pilot managed to get one of the skids to hit a jutting out ridge line, and chopper started to turn toward the side. The blade was making it's wop, wop sound, and I jumped off and pulled some of the wounded off enabling him to "right" the chopper. He lifted back off, and we carried the guys we pulled off back up the hill to the LZ. There was no doubt to me that God had saved me and used me to save others.

There were many close calls in Vietnam and the Lord brought me through them all. Briefly I will tell of other happenings.

A toss of a coin decided if I or my best buddy would die. We had no idea about it, and it was devastating. We were being sent out on a mission and I asked him if he wanted to get the ammo or the C-rations. He said, "Let's flip for it." I called it in the air and won. I said," I'll get the C-rations as they were in the company area, and he had to go up to the ammo dump to get our ammo. While there, a new guy playing with a trip flare blew the ammo dump up. Steve Clement lived for a couple

more days but never came out of the coma.
Another day I was walking point down a "Red
Ball" (dirt road through the jungle) and stepped
either over or just around an anti-tank mine. We
were told to take five and as I was about ten feet
off of the road when Lieutenant Lippy came up the
road stepping over it. Unfortunately his RTO
(Radio Operator) hit it and they were both blown
about ten feet in the air.

The Lieutenant survived but his RTO rained down
in pieces. I ran to the Lieutenant who was bleeding
all over, and as I almost reached him in the middle
of the road, Willie Thomas on the other side of the
road yelled at me to stop, "Mine Field" he yelled. I
froze and they had to get out to me and the
Lieutenant by using bayonets to probe for mines.

Many other events in that war made me know that
God was protecting me.

Miracles After The Baptism of the Holy Spirit

My wife and I were married almost two years after
returning from Vietnam. I had never known her
and met her about eight weeks before we married.
It is another miracle that she has put up with me

for fifty years now. I had been smoking pot for eight years, something Jackie never liked nor did. After five years of marriage I realized that I had drifted away from the Lord; not in my beliefs but just not doing anything for Him. My younger brother was after me for months to come with him to a Men's Bible Study, and I finally went. That night after watching these real believers I told them that I wanted what they had. They told me I needed the Baptism of the Holy Spirit, and I received it that night. My life changed overnight!

Two months later I literally walked out of jointly owning half of five music stores and head shops. Everyone in the Bible Study told me that God would really bless me for giving up ownership in these stores, but it was not evident at first. I took a job as a commissioned placement counselor and nearly went into financial ruin. Nine months later I became a new Chevrolet salesman, but that took time to build.

Deliverance From Financial Ruin

We were three house payments behind and the mortgage company was going to repossess the house. I went into work early before the dealership was opened, and laid my head down on my desk as I cried out to God. "Lord I have a wife and two little boys and they're planning to take our house. Please help me."

Just then a voice said, "Are you Dick McBain?" I looked up and saw a shadow of a man standing at my cubicle door with the sun shining brightly behind him through the showroom window. "Yes I am", I said as I was trying to see him. "I want to buy this Corvette", he said nonchalantly. I sat him down and did the paperwork and made all three house payments on that sale. I never saw the man again and had never seen him before. Think what you want, but I believe it was an angel.

Miracle of the Cesspool

Later that summer I noticed that our sewer was backing up in our backyard. I tried to ignore it but it kept getting bigger. I had just made enough money to get everything caught up but had no more. As a cesspool grew I called one of my best friends who was a plumber who came out to assess the situation. "Dick your large trees in your side yard have encroached the pipes, and you will need to replace all of the piping from the house to the street", he told me.

"John, I have no money", I told him. "Well I'll do all the labor with your help for nothing but you'll have to buy the materials", he stated. "John, I have no money", I repeated. "Well what are you going to do?" he asked. "I'm going to trust God!" I told him. "What?" he asked. "I said that I'm going to trust God", I repeated. I think he thought that I had gone crazy. We were both Catholics and had gone to Catholic schools together, but he knew nothing about the Baptism of the Holy Spirit.

When John left, Jackie asked me what we were going to do and I told her that we were going to trust God. "What?" she asked. "Honey we have no other choice, and God said in His Word that He would meet our needs with His riches in Glory by Christ Jesus", I told her. She was a bit speechless but that was that. I went into our basement and laid hands on the sewer pipes there and said, "Be open in the name of Jesus!" Nothing happened.

Over the next couple of weeks the cesspool grew quite large and deep right under our bedroom window. We had no air conditioning and it was

July. The cesspool stunk and neighbors began
complaining. I came home every night from work
and went out to the cesspool praying and reading
the Word of God to it. Jackie called several of my
best friends who came over and saw me sitting at
the edge of the cesspool, talking to it in Jesus name
and told her I had lost my mind.

After a while longer with it deep and large with all
kinds of goodies in it the miracle happened. When
I got up in the morning I walked past the window
to get my suit for work, and my peripheral vision
spotted it. I walked backward quickly and looked
out of the window. The cesspool was gone;
completely gone.

I ran out to the backyard and literally crawled
through the grass where it had been trying to find
some evidence that it had been there. There was
nothing; no paper residue or anything else there.
The grass was the same height and color as the
rest, and it was gone! It had not rained, and from
one night to the next morning it was gone. The
angels came and cleaned it up during the night, and
it was completely gone. Not only that but the pipes
were opened and we never had another problem
with our sewer system.

God Speaks To Me

Shortly thereafter I was reading the Bible in my living room, and while praying I asked the Lord why these things were happening this way. Much to my surprise He answered me and I heard him say, "Son have you ever heard of the way that they used to temper steel in the older days?" I answered out loud, "No Lord I have not!" He said, "They would take the steel and put it into the fire, pull it out and beat on it with hammers, and continue that process back and forth until the steel was much harder than before; that's what I'm doing with you; I tempering your steel; your faith!" I replied, "Thank you Lord for that." I was ecstatic!

Jackie's Foot Healed Instantly

I was working at the Chevy Dealership one afternoon when Jackie called me practically screaming in the phone. "I was moving a bookcase and the top portion fell off with all of the books in it right on my instep and has crushed it; it is so swollen and all black and blue and oh it hurts so bad", she said to me. Now my wife has a very high threshold for pain so I knew that this was bad. I told her I was on my way, and hung up.

151

I ran across the showroom floor and began praying out loud in tongues. I jumped in my car and headed out. We lived about ten minutes away and I continued praying in the Spirit. As I got close to home a miracle happened. "Foomp" went the vision up on my windshield. There before me was Jackie's foot crushed the healed right before my eyes. I ran into the house and exclaimed, "Honey your foot is healed in the name of Jesus!" She said, "No you should see it, its huge and black and blue." She had managed to put it up and get a towel over it. I yanked the towel off of her foot and it was totally healed; looked just as it should, and Jackie did a double take. She was thrilled that the Lord had healed her.

Deliverance From Devastating Theft

A year later we decided to move to Houston, Texas where my brother Bob had convinced me to come and open a trucking company with him. Houston was flourishing while the rest of the country was in a severe recession, so we decided to go. We sold the house, and I rented the largest truck that I could drive, and left in the evening. We decided to stop in Shepherdsville, Kentucky just south of Louisville. We parked the truck and went into a new Best Western Motel right off of the highway.

The next morning we walked out on our balcony and I looked out at the parking lot. "Honey, where did I park our truck", I asked. Before she could answer I saw a car that I had parked next to. "That's where I parked it", I announced, "and it's gone!" We called the small town police office to which they said that they'd never find it. Everything we owned of eight years of marriage was in that truck, and all we had was our car and the clothes on our backs.

Jackie asked tearfully what we were going to do, and I told her that we will go on with our plans and the Lord will provide. We had the money from the sale of our house to get restarted, so on we went. We stayed at my Brother's house for about two weeks until we found an apartment. In the mean time I bought an old Semi truck, and told my brother that I would have to drive a Semi before we could start a company of them so I would know what I was talking about.

A few days later the FBI called me and had found our rental truck on the side of the highway in Indiana that had been set on fire. I flew up to see if anything was still salvageable, and when I opened the back of the truck, it stunk. It had been sitting in the sun in July with everything burned and soaked ash from the fire department. I made my way through the large area and it looked like all was gone. I then looked up and right in the middle of the burned out stuff were two cardboard boxes untouched with my Bible on top of them. The boxes contained all of our irreplaceable things like our pictures, my Vietnam stuff, important papers, and so on. Thank you Jesus!

On The Brink Of Being Fired – God Delivered Me

The next miracle happened when my Brother decided to move back to Dayton, Ohio. I wasn't about to keep driving a truck so I sent out resume's and was hired by the third largest staffing company at the time in the United States, owned by H&R Block. I became the Branch Manager of the Houston Office, which at the time was a Labor Pool, and I saw it as a ministry to mostly street people. It was 1981 and as the rest of the country was recovering from the Jimmy Carter debacle of the economy, it was just hitting Houston, which people had been saying was recession proof; it wasn't.

The recession hit Houston shortly after I took the job, and our sales was going down fast. The higher-ups at headquarters in Ft. Lauderdale were beginning to think that I was not the right choice to handle Houston. One morning I was looking out of my office window and talking to the lord. "Father, I need help; they're going to fire me if I don't get things turned around soon!" Right there at my window I heard the Lord say clearly, "Son, your office is about to take off!" I was astounded that God had spoken to me again, and was so sure about it I had to tell corporate.

My boss was an atheist but we had become quite friendly. I called him and said, "Ken the Lord just spoke to me and told me this office is going to take off!" "What?" was his quick response. Now they really thought that they had a problem in Houston. I had no idea what the Lord was going to do, but just knew that He was going to.

As I continued to pray I received some wisdom and decided to get on some bid lists for people who need laborers. I was put on the State of Texas bid list and began a review of different contracts. I saw that Houston paid out eight million dollars per year on crews picking up the trash on all of the highways in and around the city. I went to a pre-bid conference and found out that we needed a fifty-thousand dollar bond just to bid on a contract. We also would have to have our own fleet of trucks, and trailers for trash bags, a huge trash compactor, and tons of safety equipment.

I began by going out on the highway with binoculars and timing the crews that had the contract to go from one area on the contract to another. I priced the trucks that I would need to buy, and designed the trailers needed for the work. The crews needed a list of safety equipment, and it was all a pretty penny. After calculating everything and the costs against a bid price, I could see that this could be it.

I called corporate about this bid process and they were very doubtful. In the mean time I was receiving calls frequently from Branch Managers around the country saying, "Hey Dick you heard any more from the Lord lately?" I had become a laughing stock in the company. Nevertheless I continued on. First my boss came to see what I was doing. He was afraid to recommend the project. Next came his boss who was a heart attack waiting to happen, and he wanted nothing to do with it. We had a later argument over the phone and I got in his face and told him that he's afraid to make any decisions. He wanted to fire me, but fortunately the Vice President was on the line at the time and stopped him.

The Vice President then came and looked at everything and said he thought I had put all of this together well, but that the upfront costs of the bond, the trucks and trailer, and so forth was a huge gamble that he didn't think he could okay. He went back and told the CEO all that he had saw, and the CEO came in to see me.

I drove him around the highways and explained that God had shown me how to put all of this together. I showed him my calculations about everything. He took me to lunch and across the table from me he told me to go for it.

Now there were about six or seven contracts counted in the eight million dollars, and I was just going to bid on the largest. I got the fifty-thousand dollar bond, filled out all the parts of the large bid package, and Jackie and I went to Austin, Texas for the bid openings and awards. The room was filled with contractors who had been doing this for years, and knew all of the ins and outs of these bids.

We were so happy when all of the bids were opened and we won. I went right to a phone and called my boss and told him, "Ken in the name of Jesus we just won our bid of one million two hundred thousand dollars." He was quite for a minute the said, "Okay Dick, now we just have to make money with it." I replied, "Faith Ken, Faith", to which he said "Yeah, okay, we'll see."

I went an bought three brand new trucks, had the trailers built, got a huge trash compactor that would sit behind our building, went and bought all of the safety equipment, the chose a top foreman to oversee the three crews needed for this contract. He hired two other foremen for the other two crews. and we began.

Shortly thereafter we were making s lot of money. The Vice President called me and asked, "Dick what are we going to do with all of this money we are making?" I told him to drop it to the bottom line and pay me my bonus, which they did and it was huge.

I was no longer the laughing stock but considered a top leader in the company. I kept telling everyone that it was the Lord, and they kept trying to make me take the credit, but I wouldn't. God came through again in what seemed impossible, and gave me the wisdom to put some big project together that I had no idea how to do. A while later we won another of these contracts with Texas.

Demon Deliverance In The Office

One morning Howard Newell, my Top Foreman over the road contracts came to me pretty upset. He said, "Dick aren't you paying attention to Stan?" Stan Meadows was one of my outside sales people, and he had let Satan in and was suicidal. I taught a Bible Study in my office every Tuesday night and Stan was one of the attendees. "No Howard I had no idea", I replied. "Well you have to do something about it", he told me.

I had been involved in deliverance ministries before, but I felt unprepared. I was the leader and reluctantly went into one of my back offices to pray. I knew that God wanted me to deal with this

Richard L. McBain

so we got Stan in that back office, and I told him what I was going to do. He agreed and took a chair. Howard, who had a Doctor of Divinity Degree came in the room along with a few other Spirit-filled employees.

I began calling on the demons in Stan to name themselves. Stan became very agitated and voices started coming out of him that were not his. The demons tried to mock me and scare me, but I had the mountain moving faith gift that the Lord had given me some time ago, and I wasn't about to be scared or quieted. We worked on Stan the rest of the day and many demons came out of him. I knew that we weren't done, but all decided to go home for some rest and start back tomorrow.

The next morning three Pentecostal Pastors, including Stan's were there to back me up. During the process one of the Pastors became so scared of what he saw coming out of Stan that he ran out of the room. We continued and some of the demons became very loud which was scaring the whole building. Someone called the Houston Police who showed up, but stayed out in the hall watching what was going on through the large door window.

They had their hands on their guns and were quite scared at what they saw.

About five in the afternoon Stan and everyone else was exhausted. I knew that we had removed many demons, and some who even gave us their names, but I wasn't sure all were gone. Howard suggested that we take Stan to the emergency room as he seemed dehydrated and very weak.

The Police officers said that they would follow me, so we headed for the hospital. I heard things in my back seat and as I looked into the rearview mirror, Stans head was moving around and he was staring at me making weird noises.

After getting him in the Emergency room I told his Pastor, Bobby Brown that he would have to stay with him while I went home to get some sleep, and he agreed. In the middle of the night I woke up in the dark and felt a presence almost sitting on me in bed. I rose up and said, "Demons in the name of Jesus, get out of my house now", and off they went. Jackie knew what was going on and asked me if I was okay and I told her I was fine, and went back to sleep.

Unfortunately about four in the morning our phone rang and it was Bobby Brown who said in a panic that I needed to get to the hospital. He said while Stan was in an emergency room space, that an old man in his eighties was wheeled by the front of Stan's space. The man had IV's and was all hooked up from having a heart attack. Bobby said that as he got in front of Stans space that he sat up, pulled the IV's out of his arm and said, "I'm Satan!" Stan sat up and said no I'm Satan, and the two got into a fist fight.

I told Bobby that he was a Pentecostal Pastor and to use the Word of God to deal with it. I told him I was not coming down there and to put those demons in their place. He agreed and went to work, and that was the end of that. After Stan was released I told him to rest at home a couple of days then come back to work. I never saw or heard of any other problems with Stan.

Corporate Corruption

After five years with this company, I went with an Executive Search firm that placed only the top five percent of lawyers and doctors. The President recruited me to open a staffing division for his company. We had to move because of my "non-compete" contract with the other company. I decided on the Hartford, Connecticut area as I thought I wanted to live in New England due to its history. I was hired as the Regional Vice President.

I started by making phone calls to staffing companies in the Hartford area asking if they knew of other good staffing people that may be looking for a job. The response I got was that I would be crazy to come and open a new staffing company there as their unemployment was at 2.7%, and that none of them could find enough people to fill the job orders that they had. I told them that I don't worry about such things because God takes care of that for me.

We moved to a rental condo in a suburb of Hartford called Collinsville. I rented an office, furnished it, and hired a staff. The Branch Manager I hired, David Lingua, had some connections to Digital Computers Home Office, and although they had a four year waiting list to get on their approved vendors, we got on.

Alice Lembo became our Staffing Manager who treated applicants like her children in a region where many services treated them harshly. Within two months we were billing Digital at the level of four million dollars per year, and applicants were coming to us in big numbers. Thank you Jesus.

After eight months in Hartford, I was flown back to Houston for a Board of Directors meeting, and asked to be the Executive Vice President and COO (Chief Operating Officer) of the corporation. Everyone thought that I was the golden boy but I kept telling them that these kinds of things don't happen except by God. They were mostly Jewish so they sort of passed that off, but I kept reminding them.

We then opened a California office and another Houston Office, and the company grew by 1000% the first year I was with them. We increased the corporate staff from eight to thirty two, and things moved well; mostly!

The President and owner of the company was a top producer in Texas, and he and I became friends. Unfortunately he did not treat his employees well, and I had continual complaints from them. I was not looking for another job, but a friend of mine in Ohio put the President of a six state region of the

U.S. staffing service in touch with me. I told him I wasn't looking for a move, but he asked if he could fly to Houston to meet with me for breakfast. I reluctantly agreed. We hit it off, the offer was right, and the family agreed to move to Marietta, Georgia.

Long story short, after one year and just buying a big house, he was indicted along with a bank president for Kiting (fraudulent use of check writing and money exchange) to the tune of two million dollars. As Executive Vice President he kept me in the dark, and I was out with nothing because the FBI locked everything down. Jackie asked me what we were going to do, and I said we are going to trust God; I began to pray.

Two or three weeks later an Atlanta company who had the "Cadillac" of the staffing industry computer software hired me for a ten state region. I had used their systems when I was with my first national staffing company. After about three weeks they were having trouble with their VP of their Staffing Company, and fired him. They asked me if I would like to be the VP of that division, and I took that position.

About three or four months later I went into the financial part of the system and found that they were cheating their Workers Comp Insurance carrier out of approximately four hundred thousand dollars a year in mis-classifying workers comp codes. I called the Comptroller to my office and she walked in white faced. "Sarah, just what is going on here?" I asked. "Oh Dick, I knew that you would find this out; I'm just following orders", she said.

After she left, I went into the system and reclassified all categories to the proper amounts. The owners were soon in my office asking me what I thought I was doing. "Do you remember when you hired me that I told you that integrity was the most important aspect of my taking any position. You then answered that's why you wanted me, because that was my reputation. This is not integrity, this is stealing and is a felony that I will not be a part of!" They said that everyone did it in the industry, and I adamantly said, "Well I don't. They then said that I was either a team player or not. I responded that I don't lie, cheat and steal for myself, and I surely was not going to do it for them.

They let it go for few more months and then came up with some phony excuse to let me go. I told them that their excuse was laughable and it was really about workers comp premiums. I gave to them in writing what I wanted for severance, which was much less than most executives get because I wanted no recriminations about extortion. They agreed and I left. Jackie asked me what we were going to do, and I said that we were going to trust God.

A couple of weeks later the Vice President of a large national public company called me and said that he had heard that I had left the other company. I had earlier spoken to him about buying their software and that's how he knew. He told me that he was sending in overnight mail plane tickets to come to their Corporate Headquarters in Dallas, Texas, to interview for a Regional Vice President position of their staffing division over the eastern third of the country; I went and was hired.

After nine months or so Mike Logal, the VP who hired me, and I had become friends. He was honest like me and we were both "Company Men" wanting the best for the company, which was on the NASDAQ Exchange. I told Mike that the executives of the company, including the President were spending too much money on things that weren't advantageous to the company. He agreed and I said that I am putting in for a fifteen percent pay cut to help out. He did the same.

We began a firestorm among the executives who began calling and asking what the heck we thought we were doing. I told them that we were trying to save the company, and if they keep up this spending, the company will go down in a year. The company had started as an Employee Placement company for fees, and the old guard thought of the staffing division as a bastard son.

Mike and I put together a plan to buy the staffing division, and corporate acted favorable. I flew to Dallas for a Board Meeting to set the deal, and as I walked into the meeting room I noticed that Mike was not there. He had been fired, and as the meeting was about to start, the former CEO and founder of the company walked in with another man. He had been fired a year earlier for stealing sixty-three million dollars from the company, and never spent a day in jail.

The man he had with him was a rich young oil

man from Houston whom he had manipulated to do a hostile takeover of fifty-one percent of the stock, so he could become the CEO again. I stood up and put my papers in my briefcase. The Chairman asked me what I was doing and I said, "If that criminal is running this company, I'm out. "But we don't want you to leave", he said. "Too bad", I said and left. Once again out in the cold and Jackie asked what we were going to do? I said trust God; He has never let us down."

After a short time I started my own consulting company to the staffing industry. I wrote and copyrighted three training manuals for the industry, and started out to build my company. The jobs were few and far between, but when I worked I was paid very well. I did some international consulting, and even found myself consulting doctors about their practices, especially when it came to management and staffing.

One of the doctors wives called me a month after working there for a few days and thanked me for saving her husband from a heart attack. He was now sleeping well, and the changes I made at his office we running smoothly and he could finally let go of the management.

As I said, my consulting paid well, but it takes a while to build up a company. I was in a low spot of productivity, and fell behind on our mortgage and cars. I prayed to the Lord to help me and show me the way. Little did I know he would answer so quickly. First one of my friends in Houston sent me an overnight envelope with a check for five thousand dollars in it. I called him and told him thank you so much but I couldn't accept this gift. He told me to get rid of my pride, and take it up with the Lord. We got all of our bills caught up.

A short period later I was in my office one afternoon and my phone rang. It was Eric who had worked for me when his uncle was indicted for kiting. His mother owned the Atlanta Franchise so when her brother was indicted, they swiftly broke out the Franchise into another corporation.

He asked me if I wanted to buy his staffing company. He needed nearly one hundred thousand dollars for his annual workers compensation premium, which has to be paid upfront, and he didn't have it. I told him that I had no money, but that I would check with a few friends of mine in the industry to see if they might be interested.

The next day I spoke to Eric and told him that I didn't find any interest in the people that I called. He said, "Dick you buy it!" I reminded him that I didn't have any money to buy anything, to which he said, "I'll finance it!" "How?" I asked. "We'll find a way because I went home to Mom's house and laid prostrate on the living room floor, and God said to me, call Dick McBain!" I told Eric to let me think about it and check on a few things to see what I can do.

Now I had my own corporation called McBain & Associates, Inc., and I called my insurance carrier who was a Spirit-filled Christian and explained the situation. He was also the insurance man for Eric. He asked me if I could come up with $2,700.00, and I told him yes (I would borrow from my mother). He said well there is no guarantee that all of his business will come to your company when he shuts down, but if you do get them or even all I can begin an insurance policy very low because we don't know what business you'll get.

I called Eric and told him I could start with almost no premium for the up-front workers comp because we don't know what will happen. I said I could set up a contract and pay him out over five years for the company. We both called his clients, and most of them knew me well from when I was with his Mother's Franchise a few years ago. Almost everyone agreed to come to my company, and practically overnight I went from behind in bills to owning a multi-million dollar company; the Lord is so good!

Our Son Mike's Miracle

Both of our son's eventually worked for the company. After six years our oldest, Dan became Vice President, and Mike worked his way to Sales Manager. In July 1999, Jackie and I were in Ohio with her mother who was undergoing quadruple heart by-pass surgery. We stayed until she was released from intensive care, and two of Jackie's brothers lived there so we headed home.

In the mountains of Kentucky my car phone went off and it was our daughter-in-law, Dan's wife. She asked me to get off of the highway, which we did. We thought that maybe Jackie's Mom died, but that was not it. "Dad, Mike has been in a terrible wreck, and they had to cut him out of the car and are life-flighting him now", she said. I could hardly speak and she continued, "Dan is on his way now but they don't know if he is going to make it", she said. Jackie could see my expressions and demanded to know what was going on.

After telling her what I knew she told me to find and airport and charter a plane. I told her I had no idea where we'd find one and just headed out on the highway. We had about six hours of drive time left, and Dan and the Intensive Care Doctor called us about once an hour with updates. We were in a state of shock and prayed.

After arriving the doctor told us that it was touch and go, and that Mike may not make it. He said that he did have his age in his favor at twenty-two, and that they had to go in and drill a hole in his skull to let the bleeding pressure out. I told the doctor that God was going to heal him and he replied I hope so.

Three days later we were in the waiting room and Jackie received a call from her brother that her Mother had died. Not only did the news tear her up, but she knew that she couldn't go to her own Mothers funeral because Mike was in a Coma. It was extremely hard on her to make that choice.

173

The next three weeks Mike was in a Coma and Jackie and I practically lived at the hospital. Mike had many friends and most came up to be in the waiting room from time to time. One morning a number of his friends were there, many who had been at our house many times and had always seen me as a strong but friendly man. I came out of intensive care as the doctors told us Mike was slipping to see his friends. As I began to speak I broke down crying, something none of them had ever seen and the room grew misty. I lifted my head up and with faith said that God was going to heal Mike.

It was hard to stand strong but God helped me through. After three weeks Mike opened his eyes but was in a vegetative state. The hospital was able to get him into Shepherd Spinal Center, a world renown brain injury hospital for evaluation. After a few days they called Jackie and I in to tell us that Mike would be a vegetable the rest of his life, and that we needed to find a 24/7 nursing facility to take care of him. Jackie said no, and that he was coming home, and I reminded them that God was going to heal Mike. I believe they thought I was crazy.

A couple of days later I went in early in the morning as Jackie and I always did while on my way to work. Jackie stayed home for the first time as she was exhausted. I walked into Mike's room where they had him in a six foot eight inch crib (Mike was 6'8") and stood over him. He was drooling from his mouth and all of a sudden he opened his eyes, shook his head, and said "Hi Dad!" He was back and the nurses came running in, some crying saying that they never see this kind of thing there. God Healed him! I called Jackie and said, "He's back!"

Mike spent the next few weeks rehabbing and running up and down the corridors in a wheel chair until his legs restrengthened. He would go up to parents in the hallway with their vegetative state kids and telling them that he was the same and God healed him. He gave many parents hope for their kids, and the hospital talked about him for years after he came home.

Deliverance At The Georgia Men's Advance

Two years later I was asked by Jimmy Rogers to be on the Board of the Georgia Men's Advance Committee. The Georgia Men's Advance was started by Jimmy Rogers and Del Swiger twenty-one years before, and was a huge men's retreat. (Called an Advance because Christians don't retreat) More than two thousand men would come over two weekends. Each weekend had the same program and it went to two weekends because the facility could only handle a little over a thousand at a time.

We had a large tent on the grounds that we used as a bookstore, and gathering place after and between speakers and break-out sessions. One night after the evening program the tent was filled as usual. Dr. Doug Jarrard and I were at one end of the tent talking when the President of the Rome, Georgia Chapter of FGBMFI (Full Gospel Business Men's Fellowship International) came to us bringing a young twenty-one year old man, and asked us to deal with him; that he needed deliverance from demons.

Dr. Doug and I had both been involved in Deliverance's before, and we began to talk to this young man. He wanted something to be done for him but didn't know what. Dr. Doug took the lead and began binding the demons and calling them out. The man became very agitated and animated, so I grabbed him from behind and assured him we were only trying to help him. He and I were both six feet three inches tall, and he looked like a body builder in stature.

As Dr. Doug was calling out the demons all kinds of voices were coming out of this man in loud and derogatory language. He struggled to break out of my half-nelson grip, and managed to use his foot to knock Dr. Doug to the ground, who got right back up and continued on. The young man then projectile vomited which just missed Dr. Doug, which is a way many demons come out. The loud voices had the people clearing out of the tent for what they heard and saw, and Jimmy Rogers remained praying.

After an hour or so the young man was totally delivered of many demons. He confessed to us that he felt so free and good. He told us that he had murdered someone and had been in a bad gang. He looked so happy and kept expressing his gratitude, where we reminded him that it was the Lord and the power of the Holy Spirit that had delivered him. He accepted Jesus right then as his Lord and savior and was baptized in the Holy Spirit. We all left the tent very happy that night.

I led the morning worship service the next morning at 6:30 am, and as I walked past the tent to the Chapel across the street, I saw this young man sitting on a park bench by the tent with a huge smile on his face, and what appeared to me like a glow around him. He had been delivered of demons that ruled him for years and was so happy. He shortly thereafter joined Campus Crusade and travelled around telling how God had delivered him from hopelessness and evil works.

Deliverance In Our House

We had a family house guest in Pasadena Texas who I felt needed deliverance. Jackie and our two boys were out shopping on a Saturday, and I asked him if I could help with some of his problems. I began to tell him that sometimes demons get into us unawares and cause us problems. I told him that I would like to deal with them if he would let me, and he agreed.

I began to call out demons in the name of Jesus and felt their presence as they came out. I made a monumental mistake in not commanding them to leave the house. He accepted the lord afterwards, and things were better.

178

That next week I was at my office in downtown Houston when my secretary told me that my wife was on the phone saying it was urgent. I answered the phone and my wife was in a panic. She said that there was seven demons around her bed all dressed alike in brown Granny dresses, and were throwing her around on the bed.

I could hear the bed being lifted an dropped, and I told Jackie to hold the phone out in front of her. She held it out and I yelled, "In the name of Jesus get out of our house now!" A minute later Jackie said that they ran one by one out of our bedroom and house quickly. I had made a stupid mistake in the earlier deliverance not to tell the demons to get out of the house and stay out, but now that was dealt with. Jackie was pretty shaken but was unharmed and okay.

Another Position From Nowhere

After ten years of wonderful blessings with our company, our second largest client was bought by a big national company that had a national contract with another staffing company. Very shortly thereafter our largest client said that their largest client had moved out of state and there business to us would be drastically reduced. We lost somewhere around a Million dollars of business between them both practically overnight. I ended up selling our company to another service like ours who were national, and Dan went with the deal. Mike decided to do something else.

I went into real estate and did fairly well the first few years, and then a slow-down came into the industry. I was once again behind in bills and asking the Lord to show me the way. Shortly thereafter He did! I was sitting in my home office looking at bills when the phone rang.

"Are you Dick McBain?" the voice asked. I said yes and the man said, "My name is Fred Tucker, the President of the Association of Realtors of Cherokee County, and wanted to know if you would be interested in coming to our Board and interview for our CEO position?" I was silent for a moment then asked how he had even heard about me as I was in Cobb County. He told me that he saw my resume on the internet, and I said that I wasn't even aware that I had a resume on the internet.

After talking with Fred, I decided to go for the

interview, and was called on my phone about fifteen minutes after leaving the interview. I went back and was offered the position, and I had already told them my requirements in salary. Once again God came through from my prayers to a well paying top position. With God's help We doubled the size of the Cherokee County Realtor School, and at the time of hiring me we had fifteen hundred Realtors in Cherokee County.

All of our miracles have been a result of God's love and has nothing to do with anyone being more special than anyone else in God's eyes. He honors faith and those who will believe no matter what it looks like. Faith comes by hearing, and hearing by the Word of God. We develop our faith by reading the Word regularly and asking God to reveal His precepts to us.

Richard L. McBain

About The Authors

Richard "Dick" McBain is the author of 23 published books and is a lifelong Christian. His real passion is to spread the Word of God so people can be saved from their sins. He has been a corporate executive for thirty-five years, is a decorated combat veteran of the Vietnam War, married for fifty years with two sons (one deceased) and four grandchildren. He became a member of Full Gospel Business Men's Fellowship in 1977, is a former national officer, and now is the Atlanta Chapter President.

Douglas Raine is the National Director of Training and Outreach for Full Gospel Business Men's Fellowship in America. Doug has taken mission trips many times into forbidden countries like Iran, Red China, Ukraine, Kurdistan, Cuba, Armenia, Jordan, and many others to spread the Gospel, and relates some of these true stories in this book.

183

 **Gary Vanover** is a barber who later in life heard a calling from God to be a missionary. He travels into many times dangerous territory laden with voodoo, witchcraft, and government forbiddance to share the Gospel of Jesus. He ministers in Nicaragua, Cuba, Guatemala, Bosnia and Ghana, and has planted churches and trained team members there.

Our Testimony & The Blood Of The Lamb